Mysteries and Fantasies

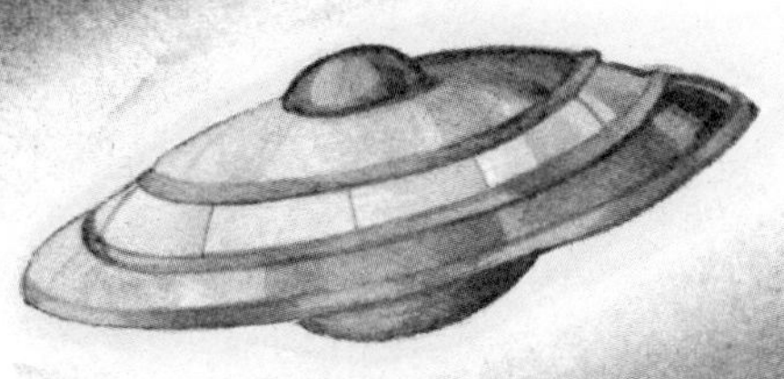

Mysteries and Fantasies

A supplement to
Childcraft—The How and Why Library

World Book, Inc.
a Scott Fetzer company
Chicago London Sydney Toronto

Merchandise Mart Plaza, Chicago, Illinois 60654

Printed in the United States of America
ISBN 0-7166-0686-0
Library of Congress Catalog Card No. 65-25105

Contents

Preface

Strange and fantastic things have always fascinated people. Long ago, people puzzled about such things as stones that seemed to fall from the sky (meteorites), and believed in such fantastic creatures as dragons and unicorns. Today, people wonder if there really is a "monster" in Loch Ness, or if UFO's could be visitors from space.

Some of the mysteries that fascinate people to this day, such as whether there are sea serpents, or whether there was an Atlantis, are thousands of years old. For some people, these and other old mysteries have never been solved satisfactorily. Other mysteries, such as black holes in space and the death of all the dinosaurs, are rather new. It almost seems that when an old mystery is solved, a new one pops up to take its place! Perhaps this is just because people *like* mysteries. Maybe it is simply that they *want* to wonder about things, even though they really know those things are fantasies.

In this book you'll find facts about several dozen famous mysteries and fantasies, old and new. You can decide for yourself which are the mysteries and which the fantasies.

Monster Mysteries

Is There Really a Loch Ness Monster?

The lake known as Loch Ness, in Scotland, is big, deep, cold, and dark. All around it are rugged, tree-covered mountains. It is just about the perfect "home" for a monster. And that's exactly what it is supposed to be—the lake in which the famous Loch Ness monster is said to live.

The oldest known story of the Loch Ness monster is more than fourteen hundred years old. It is in a book written in Scotland in the year 565. The story is about a Christian holy man who once saved a swimmer from a ferocious monster that lived in the lake. The monster is mentioned again in books written in 1520, 1827, and 1900. But not until the 1930's did people really begin to take notice of the monster of Loch Ness.

Until 1930, few people except those living near the lake had even heard of the monster. Then, in the summer of that year, three men who had been fishing on Loch Ness claimed they saw a huge animal of some sort swimming near their boat. Their story appeared in a small Scottish newspaper, but no one paid much attention to it.

Three years later, in the spring of 1933, another Scottish newspaper ran a story about Loch Ness. According to this story, two people driving past the lake had seen some kind of enormous animal rolling and plunging in the water. They watched it for a full minute, then it dived out of sight.

A month later, another man and woman claimed to have seen the creature on land. They were driving along the lake when a gigantic animal came out of the woods beside the road and crossed their path, heading for the water.

During the next few months a number of other people, one of them a minister, claimed to have seen the monster. And in November, a newspaper published what were said to be pictures of the creature. They had been taken by a man walking along the shore who happened to have a camera with him. However, the pictures were so blurry it was impossible to tell what the thing in them was, or even if it was alive.

What did all these people who claimed to have seen the monster say it looked like? Most of them said they hadn't seen it clearly enough to be sure. Some said it had a small, snakelike head on a long snaky neck. Others said it had a large head and almost no neck. But they all agreed that it was very big.

Newspapers around the world printed some of the stories of the monster. By the end of 1933, a

This photograph, taken in 1934, is the most famous picture of what is supposed to be the Loch Ness monster.

great many people had heard of the monster of Loch Ness. Many did not believe there really was a monster, but some did, and wondered what kind of creature it was. Interest in the monster began to grow.

In April 1934, another picture was taken of something in Loch Ness. The man who took the picture was a doctor and an officer of the British Army. He said he could not tell for sure what the thing he photographed was, but the picture seems to show a long neck and snakelike head sticking up out of the water. To this day, this is the best and most famous picture of what is supposed to be the Loch Ness monster—though many people say it may be nothing but a floating tree branch.

This photograph, taken in 1955, shows what looks like two large humps sticking up out of the waters of Loch Ness.

Many people have gone to Loch Ness hoping for a glimpse of "Nessie."

The picture appeared in many newspapers, and interest in the monster continued to grow. Hundreds and then thousands of people began going to Loch Ness to watch for the creature. Many of them claimed to have seen it. Many more pictures were taken of things in the lake. While none of them really showed anything clearly, several seemed to show unusual things. One shows something moving far out in the lake, leaving a broad wake, or trail of waves, behind it. Another shows two strange big bumps sticking up out of the water.

In 1968, some scientists and engineers went to Loch Ness to test a new kind of sonar—a machine that can locate things underwater by sound. These men weren't looking for the monster, and most of them didn't even believe in it. But, suddenly, the sonar began to show several very large objects moving about in the deep water of the lake!

This seemed to prove that big animals of some sort lived in Loch Ness. However, sonar often produces false shapes, known as "ghosts," exactly like the shapes shown, so there was no way to be sure. At other times when sonar was used, it usually didn't reveal anything in the lake but fish.

In 1972, an expedition from the Academy of Applied Science, in Boston, went to Loch Ness. An underwater camera with a special light attachment was lowered into the water from a boat. Every fifteen seconds the light would flash and the camera would take a picture. There was also sonar equipment on the boat.

For a week, nothing happened. Then, one evening, the sonar showed that a large shape was moving beneath the boat, near the camera. When the pictures were developed, there was something on them—a fuzzy shape. The film was put through a computer process that improved the pictures. The pictures showed what looked to be part of a big, roundish body with a large flipper, like the flipper of a sea turtle, whale, or other sea animal!

A special submarine explored the waters of Loch Ness, looking for the monster. It found nothing.

This underwater photograph shows what seems to be a flipper and part of a big body. However, the photograph was improved by a computer. The actual photograph is not at all as clear.

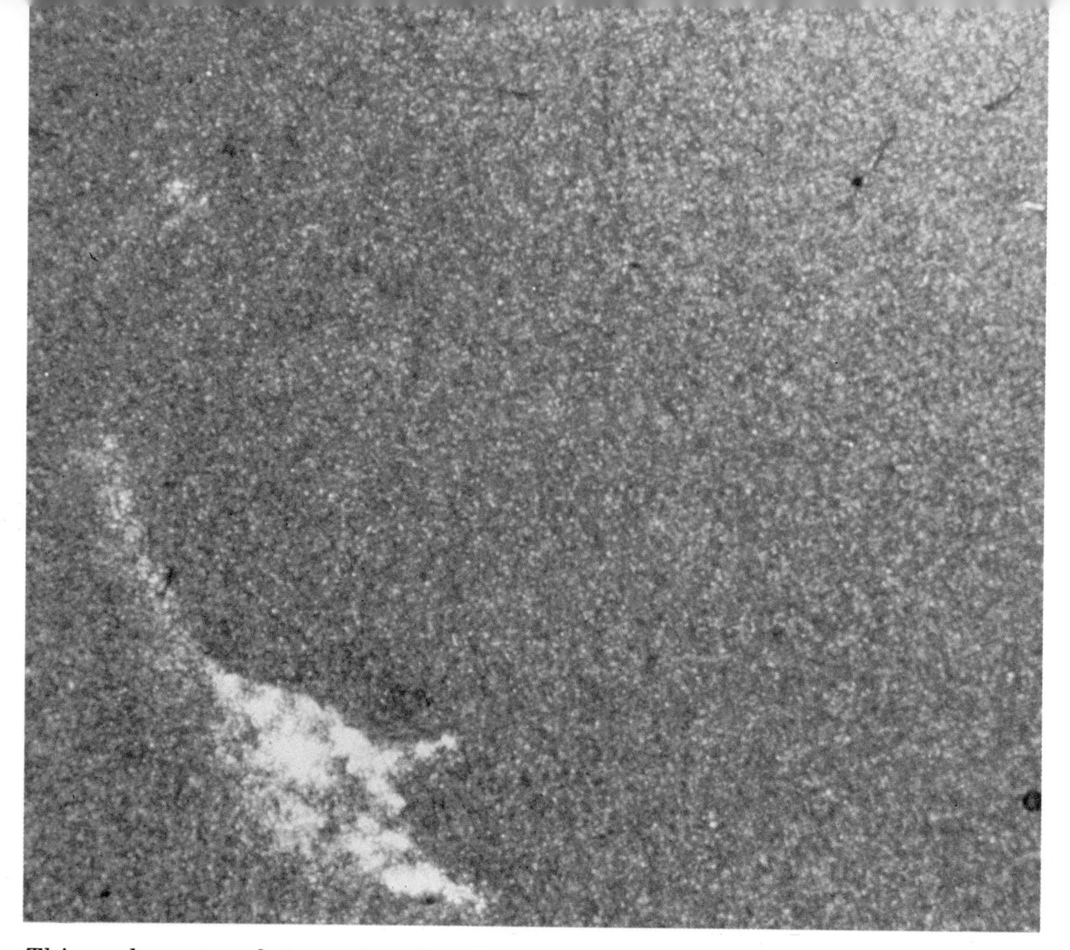

This underwater photograph, taken in Loch Ness, seems to show a long-necked animal with flippers. This photograph has been improved by a computer; the original photograph is not as clear.

The people of the Academy of Applied Science went back to Loch Ness in 1973, hoping to get more pictures. But they had no luck at all. They went back again in 1975. This time, the underwater camera took some pictures of what many people are convinced was, indeed, a large, unknown, living creature. One picture shows what seems to be part of a big body with flippers and a long, long neck. Another shows what some people think is a close-up photograph of a strange, ugly head.

But many scientists and experts who have studied the pictures carefully aren't at all sure. They say that what some people think is the animal's body and neck could just as easily be part of a tree, or even an ancient sunken Viking ship. The "head" seems to be just a shapeless blob to these people.

Since 1975, many other people have gone to Loch Ness in hopes of getting better pictures of a creature, or even capturing one. But, up to now, no clear, unmistakable picture has ever been taken. No animal, part of an animal, or trace of an animal (such as a bone, footprint, or piece of skin) has ever been found. However, many people insist they have seen a monster.

If there really *is* some kind of strange animal in Loch Ness, what could it be? To begin with, it couldn't be just *one* creature. There would have to be a whole group or family of creatures—probably at least as many as ten. Some people think there have been generations of these creatures in Loch Ness for thousands of years, just as there are generations of salmon and other kinds of fish.

Most people who claim to have seen the "monster" said it had a small head, long neck, and big, roundish body with flippers on the underside. There is no animal in the world that looks like this now, but there was once, millions of years ago. The creatures that scientists call plesiosaurs (PLEE see uh sawrz), which lived at the same time as the dinosaurs, looked exactly the way the Loch Ness creature is supposed to look. Because of this, some people think the Loch Ness animals may be plesiosaurs that have managed to survive in Loch Ness for millions of years.

But many people doubt this. For one thing, plesiosaurs were reptiles, and reptiles cannot live where it is cold—and Loch Ness is quite cold all year round. For another thing, plesiosaurs couldn't have lived in Loch Ness for millions of years

Some people think the Loch Ness monster might be a kind of giant seal, as shown above. Others think it could be a prehistoric plesiosaur, as shown below.

because it hasn't existed for millions of years. It is only about twelve thousand years old.

Some people think the animals may be some kind of very big long-necked seal or sea cow. Such animals can live in cold water, so they would be right at home in Loch Ness. But why should there be such a seal in Loch Ness and nowhere else in the world?

What do scientists say about the Loch Ness monster? Some scientists think there are big, unknown creatures of some sort living in the lake. But most scientists don't agree. And they have some good reasons.

These scientists point out that wherever there are groups of creatures—such as hippopotamuses, alligators, or turtles—living in a lake or swamp, they are easy to see and easy to take pictures of. They leave footprints when they come onto land. And when they die, their bodies often wash onto shore and can be found. In other words, there is always plenty of *evidence* that they really exist.

But this certainly isn't true of the Loch Ness creatures. Although many people claim to have seen them on land, no footprints have been found. No bodies have washed ashore. No piece of skin or even a single bone has been found. For more than fifty years, thousands of people have been trying to get a good, clear photograph of one of the creatures—but in all that time, no one ever has. People have tried to catch one of them with all sorts of special traps. Not one has ever been caught.

Scientists say this is simply because the creatures don't exist. If they did, *some* real proof of them would have been found by now. They have been hunted by people in boats, by divers, and by submarine. They have been searched for with sonar, computers, and underwater cameras. But after more than fifty years, there still isn't a single piece of real evidence that they exist. Perhaps the only way to prove there are no monsters in Loch Ness is to drain all the water out of it!

There is no denying that many honest, intelligent people claim to have seen strange things in Loch Ness. And no one can say for certain that there aren't any unknown animals in Loch Ness. So, as long as some people think there really is something in the lake, some of them will keep trying to find it.

The Mysterious Wild "Ape Men"

A man named William Roe was hunting in Canada one day in 1955. Tramping along through the quiet wilderness, he came out of a little patch of trees. Then, suddenly, he stopped short. Not far away, stood a large furry creature.

At first, Mr. Roe thought the creature was a grizzly bear standing upright on its two back legs. But the longer he looked at it, the more astounded he became. For, as he later told newspaper reporters, he realized that it wasn't a bear at all—it looked like a giant, thick-chested human, covered with dark brown fur! Its nose was flat, its lips stuck out, and its eyes were small and dark. It caught sight of Mr. Roe and stared at him for a moment. Then it turned and, walking upright like a human, strode off into the nearby woods.

In 1983, a Chinese schoolteacher, Mr. Li Mingzhi, was living in a village near a thick forest in Yunnan, China. Late one night, many of the village dogs began to bark in an angry, excited way. Mr. Li thought perhaps some wild animal was prowling about in the village. He picked up his hunting rifle and stepped outside.

It was a bright, moonlit night. Mr. Li looked around and saw a figure coming toward him.

Thinking it was one of his neighbors, he went to meet it—and suddenly found himself face-to-face with a huge hairy creature that was both humanlike and apelike! Mr. Li and the creature stared at each other for a few moments. Then the creature turned and scurried off toward the forest.

Stories of the sort told by Mr. Roe and Mr. Li have come from many parts of the world—the United States, Canada, China, Russia, India, and elsewhere. Thousands of people claim to have encountered strange, hairy, humanlike or apelike creatures in some lonely, wild place!

Tales of such creatures aren't new. Hundreds of years ago, many of the Indian tribes living in the northwest part of North America told tales of huge, hairy, humanlike beings that roamed the mountain forests. The Indians called them Sasquatch, and believed they had supernatural powers.

Americans and Canadians first began to hear of such creatures a little more than a hundred years ago. A story in a Canadian newspaper in 1884 told of a strange creature that had been captured near the town of Yale, British Columbia. It was said to be like a small man, about five feet (152 centimeters) tall, covered with thick hair, and tremendously strong. No one now knows what became of this creature, or what it might have been.

Ever since then, many stories of such wild, hairy, two-legged creatures have been told. A man who had once been a miner claimed that he and other miners working in a canyon in the state of Washington had fought a battle against a group of hairy, apelike things. A man who had been camping in Canada claimed that he was held prisoner for a time by a family of giant, apelike creatures. During the last thirty years or so, almost every American and Canadian has heard such stories.

A good many footprints said to have been made by the apelike creatures have been found. They look much like human footprints, but they are enormous—as much as sixteen inches (41 cm) long. Because of this, the creatures have become known as "Bigfoot."

From all the stories and footprints, people have formed an idea of what a "Bigfoot" is supposed to look like. A full-grown one is said to be more than seven feet (213 cm) tall, with wide, powerful shoulders and almost no neck. It is covered with reddish-brown furry hair, and its face resembles the face of an ape. However, its feet are very much like the feet of a human.

The mountainous lands of Tibet, Nepal, Sikkim, and Bhutan, in the Himalaya between China and India, have also long had stories of big, hairy, apelike beings. These creatures are said to live in caves high up in the mountains, and to roam the snow-covered mountainsides by night. In Nepal the creatures are called *Yeti*, which means "all-devouring demon." They are also known by the Tibetan name of *Metoh-kangmi*, meaning "Abominable [hateful and disgusting] Snowman."

They are supposed to be meat-eaters, preying on the animals that live in the mountains. And, it is said that they sometimes also prey on people!

These creatures are usually described as being about six feet (183 cm) tall and covered with reddish hair. Rows of footprints said to have been made by *Yetis* have been found on the mountainsides. And several Buddhist monasteries in the mountains have pieces of skin said to have been taken from the heads of dead *Yetis*.

In China, there are tales, thousands of years old, of creatures called *Ye-ren*, which means "Wild Man." In recent years, there have been hundreds of reports from people who claim to have seen these creatures. *Ye-ren* are said to be about seven feet (213 cm) tall, with grayish-red hair covering their bodies. Footprints and clumps of hair said to have come from *Ye-ren* have been found in places where people have reported seeing the creatures.

The land known as Russia, or the Soviet Union, is enormous. There are many wilderness areas. From the region of the Caucasus Mountains, near the Russian border with Turkey, have come tales of wild, hairy, humanlike or apelike creatures.

Farther east, in the mountains called the Pamirs, there are said to be similar creatures. There are also many stories of very tall, black-furred, apelike creatures living in the forests of the cold, snowy region of Siberia.

Bear footprints in melting snow have been mistaken for giant apelike footprints.

Dr. Grover Krantz of Washington State University displays casts of what are said to be the footprints of "Bigfoot."

In the land of Mongolia, which lies between Siberia and China, these creatures are known as *Almas*, meaning "Wild Man." They are said to be about as tall as an average human, and to have reddish-black fur. Unusual footprints have been found in most of the places where the creatures are said to live.

Thus it seems as if the world is full of some kind of unknown apelike creature or creatures. But—is it? Do these creatures really exist, or are they just a legend?

Although thousands of people claim to have seen a Bigfoot, or *Yeti*, or *Ye-ren*, or *Almas*, not one of these creatures has ever been brought, dead or alive, for scientists to study. Special expeditions of trained scientists have gone into the parts of China, Russia, and the Himalaya where the creatures are said to live, and have found nothing—not a skeleton or even a single bone. This is most unusual, for trained, experienced scientists can usually find what they go after—unless there's simply nothing to be found!

And so, a good many scientists—probably most—don't believe there really are such things as Bigfoot, *Yeti*, *Almas*, or any other such creature. They feel that if there really were thousands of these creatures in many parts of the world, at least *one* should have been found by now. They believe that people who claim to have seen these creatures are simply either telling untruths, or else just saw an ordinary animal, such as a bear, and thought it was something else.

But, what about the footprints and clumps of unusual fur? What about the pieces of *Yeti* skin in the Buddhist monasteries? What about photographs that have been made of some of the apelike creatures? Doesn't evidence such as this prove that the creatures exist?

Scientists have shown that some of the footprints are simply fakes. Others are actually the footprints of bears or other animals. Some were dog tracks in snow, melted out of shape by the heat of the sun.

As for the pieces of *Yeti* skin that are supposed to be from the heads of dead *Yetis*, one of these was examined by scientists. They found that it was a piece of stretched skin from the body of a mountain goat.

In 1967, a man took some motion pictures, in color, of a Bigfoot he claimed to have encountered in a wild part of northern California. In the film, the tall, hairy creature is seen moving away from the camera, turning partway to look back before it moves out of sight into some thick woods. The film was carefully examined by a number of scientists from the United States, Canada, and Europe. Most of them felt that the "Bigfoot" was really a person dressed up in a furry costume. There were things wrong with the way the creature looked and the way it walked that only scientists who had studied many apes would have known about. Most scientists think the film is a fake, but a very clever one.

So, some of the "evidence" for Bigfoot and the *Yeti* is nothing more than fakes and mistakes. On the other hand, there is some evidence which, most scientists agree, seems to be real! There are some footprints, apparently made by a Bigfoot with a crippled foot, that do not seem to be fakes. And some of the hair of a *Ye-ren*, which was examined by a Chinese scientist, was found to be completely different from the hair of any known animal!

A few scientists think that Bigfoot and some of the other wild, hairy "ape men" really do exist. They think there simply couldn't be so many stories and so much puzzling evidence if the creatures weren't real. Some of these scientists

The man who took this film claims that it shows a Bigfoot. But most scientists think it is just a person dressed in a costume.

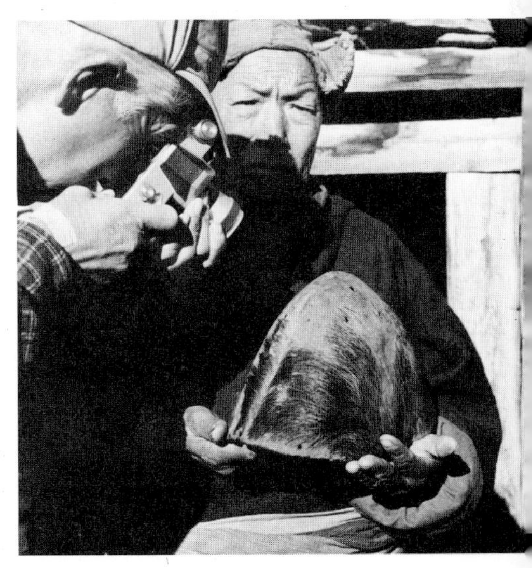

Scientists found that what was said to be a Yeti *scalp is actually just a piece of skin from a mountain goat.*

think the creatures are probably some kind of ape that belongs to the same family as gorillas, chimpanzees, and other apes. But a few scientists think that some of the creatures may be descendants of "cave people" who have been hiding away from other humans for thousands of years!

Thus, at this moment, no one is really quite sure whether the "ape men" exist or not. If, in the next few years or so, a live or dead Bigfoot or *Yeti* or *Ye-ren*—or even the bones of one—is brought to scientists for examination, that will be all the proof that's needed. But if more and more time goes by without any of these creatures actually being found, most people will have to agree that the stories of big, mysterious, apelike beings are, indeed, just stories.

Are There Still Dinosaurs in Africa?

Some sixty-five million years ago, much of the world's land was covered with hot, humid jungle and swamp in which the gigantic reptiles we call dinosaurs lived. Today, in Africa, in the People's Republic of the Congo, there is a vast hot and humid area covered with thick forests and dotted with streams and swamps. This land probably hasn't changed much since the time of the dinosaurs. One part of this area, which has hardly been explored, is inhabited only by tribes of primitive Pygmies. This land is said to be the home of strange, huge animals that some people think could actually be "leftover" dinosaurs!

The Pygmies, and people of other tribes living near this part of the forest—which is known as the Likouala—call these creatures *Mokele-mbembe* (moh KAY lee muh BEM bee), which means, "one who eats the tops of palm trees." These people claim that a *Mokele-mbembe* is about the size of an elephant, with smooth, grayish-brown skin, a long, snakelike neck and head, and a long, thick tail much like the tail of a crocodile. The creatures are said to spend most of their time in the waters of the Sanga and Ubangi rivers, and to wade up onto the riverbanks at dawn or dusk to eat the fruit of a vine that grows along the rivers.

However, even though the *Mokele-mbembes* are plant-eaters and not meat-eaters, they are said to be very dangerous. The people who live near them say that if a *Mokele-mbembe* encounters a canoe full of people, it will smash the canoe and kill the people, even though it will not eat them.

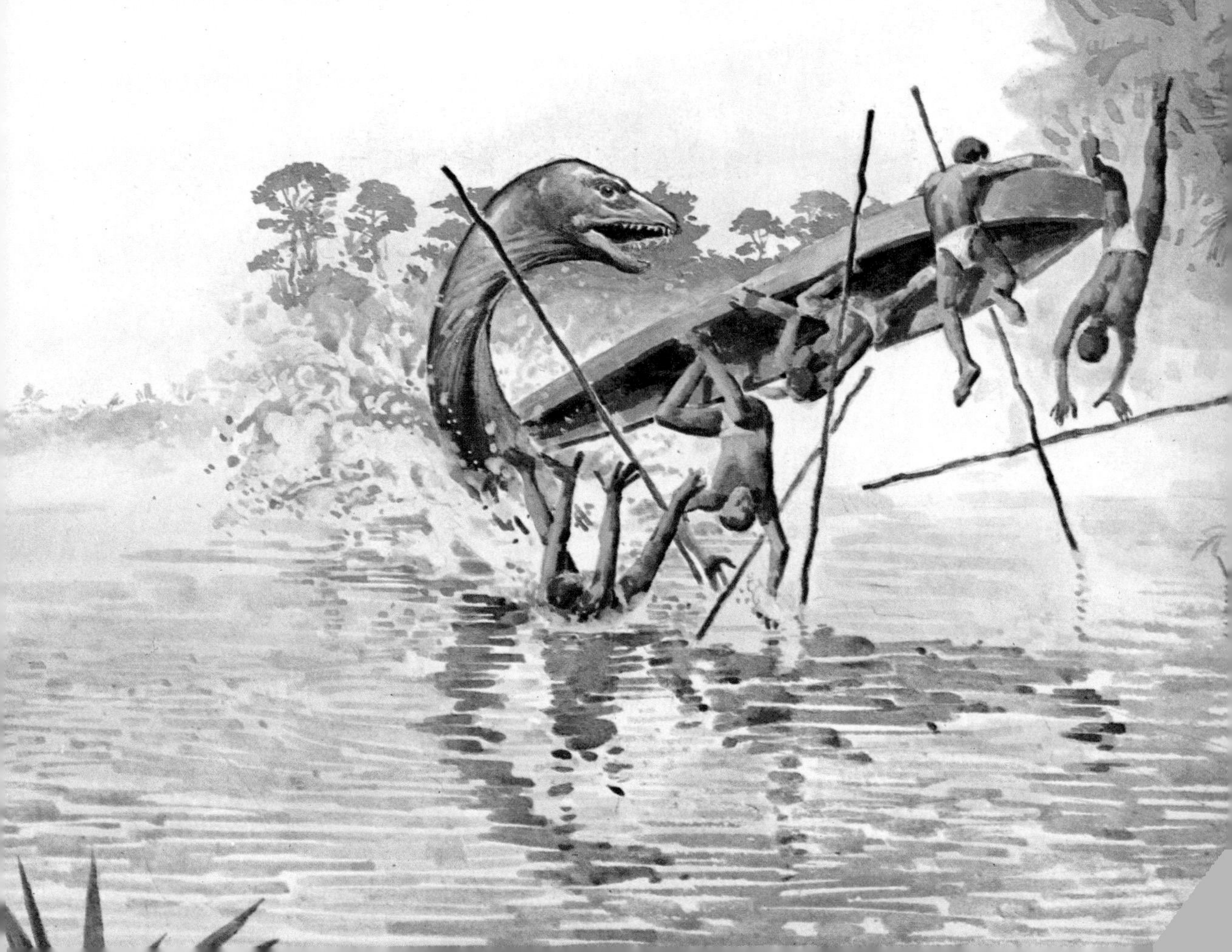

People in lands outside Africa first learned about these creatures in 1913, when a German explorer reported stories of *Mokele-mbembes* he had heard in the Congo. A few scientists noticed that the description of the creatures made them sound much like sauropod (SAWR uh pahd) dinosaurs. Sauropods were the giants of the dinosaur world. These plant-eaters averaged about seventy feet (21 meters) long and stood twelve to fifteen feet (3.7 to 4.8 m) tall at the hips. They walked on four heavy legs and had a long neck and long tail.

As time passed, some scientists and explorers tried to find out more about these mysterious *Mokele-mbembes*. In 1932, a British scientist exploring near the Likouala region where the creatures are said to live, came across some huge footprints. Later, when he went down one of the rivers in a canoe, he heard strange sounds but did not see anything. In recent years, a scientist studying crocodiles near the Likouala photographed a huge, clawed footprint thirty-six inches (91 centimeters) wide. In 1978, a group of French explorers went into the Likouala region and have not been heard from since.

In 1980, an American scientist, Dr. Roy Mackal, went to the Congo to see what he could find out about *Mokele-mbembe*. He visited people who live near the Likouala region and found more than thirty who claimed to have actually seen a

Mokele-mbembes are said to look like a prehistoric sauropod dinosaur, such as the one shown here.

Mokele-mbembe. Dr. Mackal had brought along a number of pictures of animals such as elephants, hippopotamuses, and crocodiles, as well as some pictures of sauropod dinosaurs. When he asked people who said they had seen a *Mokele-mbembe* to pick out the animal that was most like it, they all chose one of the dinosaur pictures.

Dr. Mackal decided to form an expedition to try to find and photograph, or even capture, a *Mokele-mbembe*. In October of 1981, he and two other scientists, with a professional photographer and other people, headed into the steamy, swampy

Dr. Roy Mackal and his party are shown as they set off on the second Likouala expedition in an unsuccessful search for the Mokele-mbembe.

jungle of the Likouala. They spent six weeks searching, but found no trace of anything such as a *Mokele-mbembe*, except for a trail of footprints and crushed grass leading to a river. The trail could have been made by an elephant, but it looked to some of the men as if some of the grass had been flattened by a long, heavy tail dragging through it.

At the very same time, another expedition was also in the Likouala, searching for a *Mokele-mbembe*. However, there were no trained scientists with this group. In December of 1981, the head of this expedition sent word that he and some of the others had actually seen a creature that seemed to be a sauropod dinosaur, and that they had taken a picture of it. But when the expedition returned to the United States, the leader said that the photographic film had been spoiled by the heat of the jungle and there was no picture after all.

And so, neither expedition brought back any real proof that *Mokele-mbembes* actually exist. Most scientists think they probably do not—that the stories of people seeing a *Mokele-mbembe* are simply made-up "monster tales," like so many others from all parts of the world. Unless an expedition actually brings back some clear photographs, some bones, the body of a *Mokele-mbembe*, or a living one, most scientists will doubt that there are "leftover" dinosaurs living in Africa.

Mysteries of Space

Is There a Planet X?

One of the first things everyone learns about the solar system is that there are nine planets circling around the sun—Mercury (MUR kyuhr ee), Venus (VEE nuhs), Earth, Mars, Jupiter (JOO puh tuhr), Saturn (SAT uhrn), Uranus (yu RAY nuhs), Neptune (NEHP toon), and Pluto (PLOO toh). However, a great many astronomers believe there's a tenth planet that hasn't been found yet. They call it "Planet X."

Why do astronomers think there's a tenth planet when no one has ever found any trace of it? Well, there's a very good reason. They haven't seen the planet, but they have seen its gravity at work.

Everything in space has gravity—a force that pulls. Even across many millions of miles (kilometers) of space, the tug of a big planet's gravity may be strong enough to have an effect on a smaller planet. Astronomers have known for a long time that there is an "extra" tug of gravity in the solar system—a tug that may be coming from an undiscovered planet.

This tug of gravity was first noticed more than

two hundred years ago, soon after an astronomer discovered Uranus, the seventh planet in the solar system. Uranus is about 1.8 billion miles (2.9 billion km) from the sun. When astronomers figured out Uranus' orbit—the path it takes around the sun—they found that the orbit bulged way out on one side. It was just as if something were pulling at Uranus strongly enough to tug it out of its regular path.

Astronomers thought that a large planet would be the most likely thing to pull strongly on Uranus, so they started looking in the direction the pull was coming from. Sure enough, they soon found another planet. This was Neptune, the eighth planet, about 2.8 billion miles (4.5 billion km) from the sun.

However, Neptune isn't really big enough to give such a strong tug to Uranus. Besides, something seemed to be tugging at *it*. So astronomers figured there must be another planet even farther out. They searched and searched—and after a long, long time, they found the ninth planet, Pluto. It is about 3.7 billion miles (5.9 billion km) from the sun.

But Pluto is just a "runt" of a planet, a little smaller than Earth's moon. The pull of its gravity isn't great enough to account for the strong tugs on Uranus and Neptune. This is why many astronomers think there must be a huge tenth planet beyond Pluto—Planet X.

If there is a Planet X, it may be as much as 5 billion miles (8 billion km) from the sun. It would get very little sunlight to reflect, so it would be very dim and hard to see. Some astronomers think it may be a "brown body"—a huge globe of gas that doesn't reflect much light. That would make it very hard to find.

But, hard to find or not, many astronomers are searching for Planet X. If it is there, they'll find it sooner or later!

Is There Life in Space?

On an October night in 1938, terror filled the hearts of thousands of people on the East Coast of the United States. They believed that invaders from the planet Mars had landed and were about to conquer the world!

Of course, no such invasion took place. A radio broadcast of a famous story—*The War of the Worlds*—caused the scare. It was so realistic many people thought Earth had actually been invaded. At that time, no one knew what the planet Mars was like. Some scientists thought there might be living creatures there. The idea of "men" from Mars attacking Earth seemed possible.

Could creatures from another planet ever attack Earth? Are there other living things in space?

People once believed that most of the planets of the solar system were probably much like Earth. Many astronomers thought that the planet Venus was a swampy jungle, perhaps filled with dinosaurlike animals. They believed that the planet Mars had water and plant life—grass and trees—and was crisscrossed with long canals that might have been dug by intelligent creatures! So little was known about the planets Jupiter, Saturn, Neptune, and Uranus that people thought they, too,

might have water and vegetation, and could support animal life.

Today we know a great deal about most of the planets of the solar system. We know that the planet Mercury, closest to the sun, is a barren ball of rock, like Earth's moon. Venus is a waterless, rocky desert, so hot that a piece of lead placed on the surface would melt! Mars is also a rocky desert, but it is so cold that most of its water is frozen into masses of ice at its north and south poles. There are no canals. And space probes sent to Mars to look for life found no proof of any living thing.

As for Jupiter and Saturn, both of these planets are now known to be gigantic balls of fluid. Neptune and Uranus are probably fluid, too. It is doubtful that any living things exist on any of these planets. The planet Pluto is probably a barren, rocky ball like Mercury. It is so far from the sun that almost no light or warmth reaches it. Thus, most scientists feel quite sure there are no living things on any planet in the solar system except Earth.

Scientists don't think there is much chance that anything lives on any of the moons of the solar system, either. There are about fifty moons. Some of them are as big as, or bigger than, the smallest planets. But most of the moons are bare, airless balls of rock or frozen snow. One moon of Saturn, Titan, has an atmosphere made up mostly of

People once thought that dinosaurlike creatures might live on the planet Venus.

nitrogen gas, and it might have lakes of a chemical called methane. But while there *might* be some form of life on Titan, it seems impossible that any intelligent creatures might live there or on any of the other moons.

So, if there is life in space, it must be out beyond the solar system—among the trillions upon trillions of stars in the universe. Surely, among so many

People once believed that intelligent creatures lived on Mars. In the book, The War of the Worlds, *Martians invade Earth.*

stars, there must be many that have "families" of planets, as the sun does. And surely, among all those planets, there might be many that, like Earth, swarm with living things.

At one time, not very long ago, most scientists thought so. In fact, it was believed there were probably billions of planets like Earth scattered all over the universe. Now scientists aren't so sure. Many of them think a planet such as Earth, which is full of life, could be very, very rare.

Science-fiction movies show many kinds of space creatures, as in this scene from Return of the Jedi.

In the book Out of the Silent Planet *by C. S. Lewis, a man goes to Mars and finds several kinds of intelligent creatures. But space probes have found no proof of life on Mars.*

But even if there were many planets like Earth, with living things on them, how many of those planets would have intelligent living things such as humans? Some scientists think that intelligent creatures like us, who have invented such things as radio and television and spacecraft, may also be very, very rare.

This huge radio telescope near Arecibo, Puerto Rico, collects and measures radio waves given off by objects in space. A computer turns the radio waves into pictures.

Is there any way we can find out if there are other intelligent creatures in the universe? For that matter, is there any evidence for any kind of life at all beyond the planet Earth?

There is some slight evidence for life in space. Many meteorites—chunks of rock from space—have fallen to Earth. On some of these, scientists have found traces of the kinds of chemicals that form living things. Thus, we know that the chemicals necessary for life exist in other parts of space. This tells us that life *could* arise somewhere else besides Earth. But it does not prove that there is life elsewhere.

As for finding out if there are intelligent creatures elsewhere, there are ways of doing that. Scientists are trying some of these ways. For a number of years, big radio telescopes—instruments that can pick up radio waves from space—have been "listening" for signals. If there is another planet with intelligent creatures on it, those creatures, too, may be searching for intelligent life. They may be sending out radio messages in the hope that someone will hear them. Our radio telescopes could pick up such a message.

Scientists call this search for other life SETI (SEHT ee), which stands for "search for extraterrestrial intelligence." *Extraterrestrial* (ehks truh tuh REHS tree uhl) means "beyond Earth." Most of those working on SETI feel sure

Motion pictures such as E.T.: The Extra-Terrestrial *tell stories of visits to Earth by creatures from outer space.*

that, sooner or later, other intelligent life will be discovered.

But a great many scientists just don't think so. One scientist has estimated that planets such as Earth, with intelligent life, would be at least 19.2 trillion miles (30.9 trillion kilometers) apart in space. It would take millions of years for radio signals to cross such an enormous distance.

And some scientists think there may not even be any other intelligent creatures in the universe. They think we may be the only ones.

These scientists point out that just as some stars are known to be older than others, many planets are bound to be older than others. If there were other planets with intelligent creatures, some of those planets would be far older than Earth. The creatures living on them would have had a long time to learn things. They would be hundreds, or even thousands, of years ahead of us in space travel, communications, and everything else. If there were such creatures, we would surely have been visited by them, or would have heard from them, by now.

So, we really don't know if there is life in space. Some scientists think there is, and are searching for signs of it. Others don't think so. All that can be said for sure is that it is possible.

Are There "Holes" in Space?

Space is nothingness. There are things *in* space—stars, planets, drifting gas and dust, waves of light, and so on—but space is just nothingness, or emptiness, in which those things exist.

Yet, you may have heard that scientists say there are things called "black holes" in space. How can there possibly be a hole in *nothing*?

Scientists explain it this way: There are different sizes of stars. All stars are enormous, but some are enormously enormous! There are stars a thousand times bigger than our sun, which is 109 times the size of Earth. All stars have tremendous gravity, of course, and the more matter a star has, the more gravity it has.

Stars change, just as everything else does. When a lot of the matter in a star has been used to make heat and light, the star begins to die. A very big star will suddenly collapse. Its gravity instantly pulls every bit of what is left of the star in toward the middle. As gravity keeps pulling, all of the matter squeezes tighter and tighter, into a ball. The bigger the star, the more tightly it squeezes together. Scientists know that many gigantic stars collapse into balls no bigger than Earth. Bigger stars get even smaller than that! And the more tightly their matter squeezes together, the stronger the pull of their gravity.

Many scientists think that when the very biggest

kinds of stars collapse, their enormous gravity squeezes them together so tightly that almost nothing is left but the gravity itself! A kind of whirlpool of gravity is formed, with such a tremendous pull that even things that are quite far away are affected by it. And nothing that is pulled into this enormous field of gravity can get away—not even light, which is the fastest-moving thing there is. And if none of its light gets out of

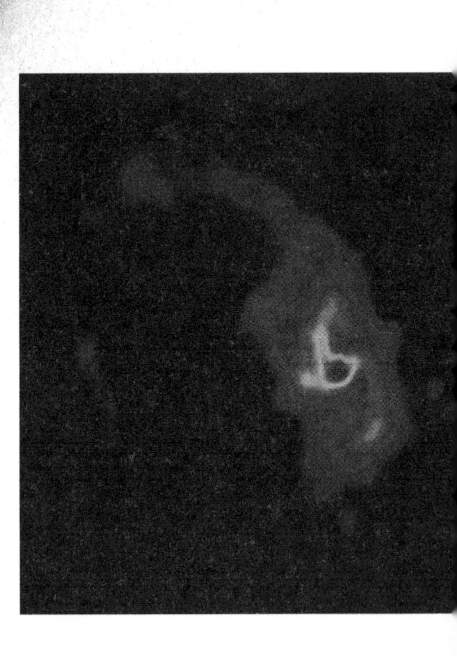

The tremendous gravity of a black hole (left) *would pull gas from a nearby star. The picture* (right), *taken by radio telescope, shows what may be the center of our galaxy, where there is thought to be a black hole.*

the gravity field, the collapsed star can't be seen—it will be invisible. For this reason, scientists call such a field a "black hole."

Now, if a black hole is invisible, how can scientists tell there are such things?

There is a way. If a black hole lies near a large star, its gravity should have an effect on that star. Astronomers have found several stars that look as if they were affected by a black hole.

One of these stars is in a galaxy known as the Large Magellanic (maj uh LAN ihk) Cloud. Astronomers can tell that gas is being pulled out of this star by a tremendous tug of gravity from nearby. Such a strong tug could only come from a huge star or a black hole. Of course, if there were a nearby star, astronomers could see it. But there is no nearby star. So most astronomers are sure the tug of gravity comes from an invisible black hole.

Astronomers also feel there is good evidence for a "super" black hole in the middle of the Milky Way, the galaxy to which our sun belongs. Instruments show that something with an enormous tug of gravity causes clouds of gas to circle around this something at thousands of miles (kilometers) per hour.

Scientists aren't sure whether a black hole actually *is* a hole in space. But most scientists feel certain that black holes do exist, and that space may be full of them!

Mysteries of the Sea

Are There Sea Serpents?

For thousands of years, people have thought of the ocean as a vast, mysterious place where fantastic things could happen. There are more myths, legends, and tales about the ocean than about any other part of the earth—legends of mermaids, sea monsters, ghost ships, disappearing islands, sunken cities, and other weird and wonderful things. One of the oldest of all legends is the legend of the sea serpent—a gigantic snakelike creature said to live in the ocean.

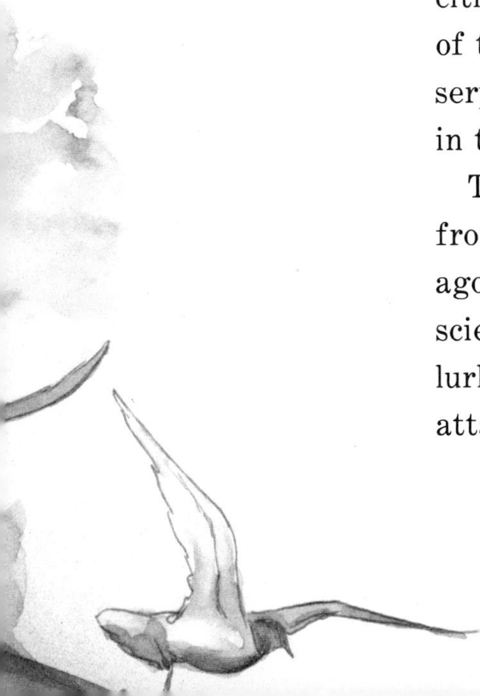

The oldest sea serpent tale we know of comes from a book written more than two thousand years ago. The author of the book, the famous Greek scientist Aristotle, tells of giant sea serpents that lurked along the coast of North Africa, and often attacked passing ships. Aristotle said the serpents would fling themselves against ships to break them to pieces. Then the serpents would eat the sailors floundering in the water!

Such tales continued to be told for centuries. In the year 1555, a book published in Sweden told of a sea serpent that was often seen off the coast of Norway. It was said to be two hundred feet (61 meters) long and twenty feet (6 m) thick, with black scales and fiery, shining eyes. According to the book, this huge serpent would pluck sailors right off their ships and devour them!

In another book, written almost two hundred years later, a Norwegian missionary told of a huge sea serpent he had seen while traveling from Norway to Greenland. And in 1746, the crew of a Norwegian ship swore they had seen a sea serpent that had a horselike head, black eyes, and a long, white mane.

Despite such stories, by the beginning of the 1800's few people really believed in sea serpents. But then, in 1817, a large number of people in Gloucester, Massachusetts, saw what appeared to be a huge, snakelike creature with a turtlelike head swimming in the harbor. A group of scientists investigated the reports and decided that the people really had seen some kind of unusual sea creature.

In 1848, a huge snakelike creature was seen by some of the officers and crew of the British warship H.M.S. *Daedalus*. It was (and still is) the duty of a navy ship's captain to keep a record of everything that happens to his ship. So the captain of the *Daedalus* made a full report to his superiors about the sea serpent.

The captain said that the creature had passed so close to the ship that if it had been a person he knew, he would have recognized that person. He said the creature looked just like a huge snake, about sixty feet (18 m) long and fifteen or sixteen inches (38 or 41 centimeters) thick, with dark brown back and sides and a whitish underside. It was moving very fast, in a straight line.

A lot of scientists and other people who didn't believe in sea serpents were puzzled by this report, because it simply couldn't be doubted. The captain of a British warship would not dare make a false report to his superiors. Besides, several of the other officers of the *Daedalus* turned in reports of the creature. There was no doubt that they had all seen something. But had it truly been a sea serpent?

One scientist thought it might have been a very large seal. Another person thought it might even have been an African dugout canoe, carved in a way that made it look like a huge snake.

There were several other reports of sea serpents in the 1800's. In 1875, the captain and crew of a small ship heading toward Africa saw what seemed to be a death battle between a whale and a sea serpent! As the men watched, it looked as if the serpent wrapped itself around the whale and dragged it beneath the water. In 1877, the captain and crew of a British ship near Sicily saw a creature with a long body and a head like that of a crocodile. In 1893, the captain and some of the crew and passengers of a ship sailing near Africa saw a creature that resembled a gigantic eel, which is a fish that looks like a snake.

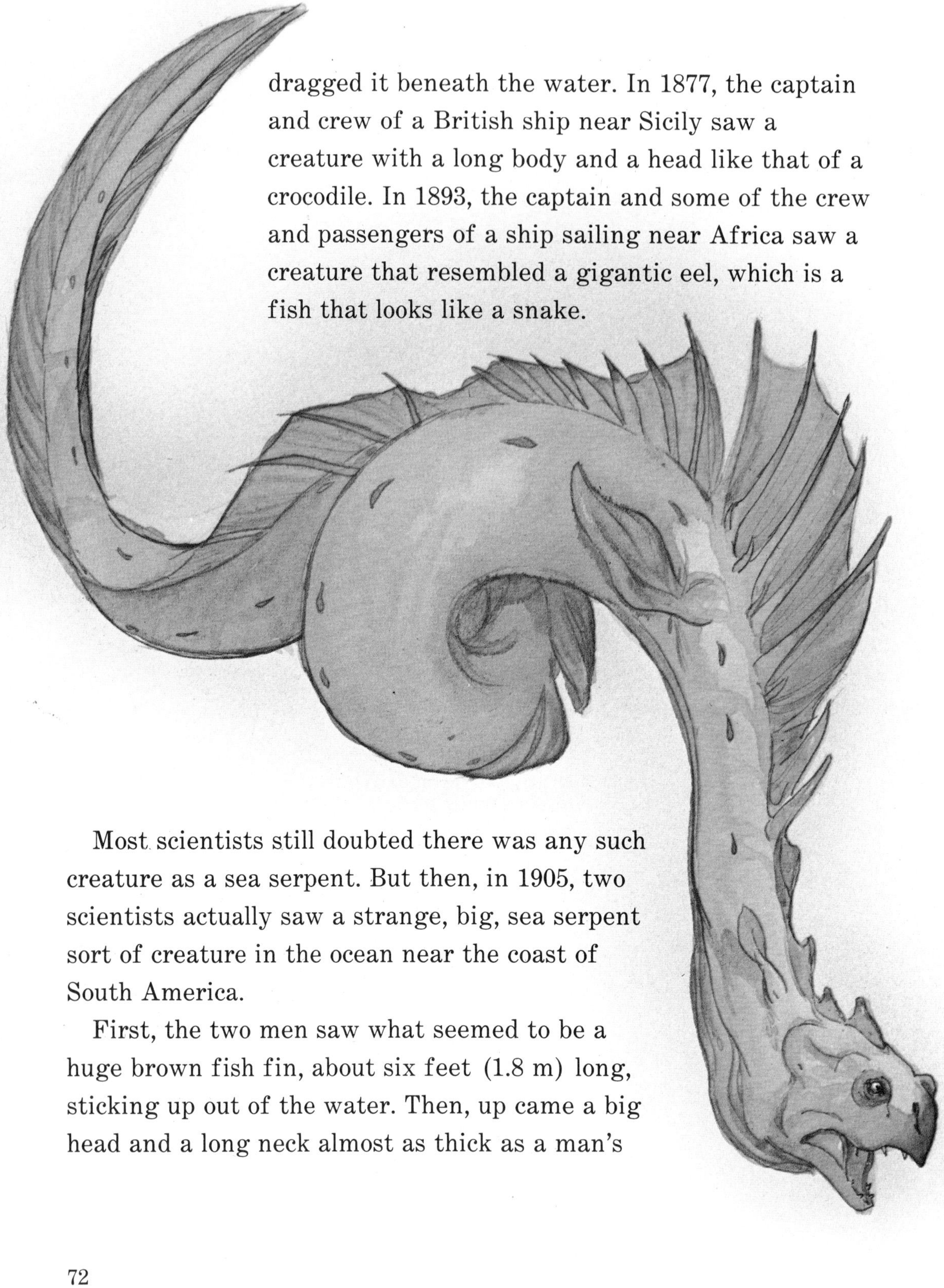

Most scientists still doubted there was any such creature as a sea serpent. But then, in 1905, two scientists actually saw a strange, big, sea serpent sort of creature in the ocean near the coast of South America.

First, the two men saw what seemed to be a huge brown fish fin, about six feet (1.8 m) long, sticking up out of the water. Then, up came a big head and a long neck almost as thick as a man's body. The head looked like the head of a turtle, and the upper part of the head and neck were dark brown, while the underside was white. One of the scientists made a sketch of the creature, and the two men gave a report of it to a scientific organization to which they belonged.

In 1913, an officer and a sailor of a steamship claimed to have seen a very strange and different sort of creature near Newfoundland. This beast had three horns on its head, ears like long fins, blue eyes, a neck twenty feet (6 m) long, and a body like a giant seal. It was yellowish-brown with brown spots.

Four years later, in 1917, the whole crew of a British merchant ship saw still another kind of creature in waters near Iceland. This beast had a long snaky body, a triangular fin on its back, and a head like a cow. It was black, with a white spot on its nose. Because World War I was going on at this time, the merchant ship was armed with a cannon, and the captain ordered the gun crew to fire at the creature. The creature was apparently hit, for it began to thresh about, and sank out of sight.

There have been a number of other reports of strange sea creatures since then, although there haven't been many in recent years. The question is, what were these creatures?

Most scientists who study the sea and its animals don't think there really is such a thing as a sea serpent. They don't believe there are any big, unknown animals living in the sea. If there were, we would have discovered them by now. The bodies of dead whales, sharks, and other big sea animals often wash ashore, so dead sea serpents should have washed ashore, too. But not one has ever been found anywhere in thousands of years.

Also, for hundreds of years whaling ships roamed the oceans in search of whales. Surely, one of them should have encountered one of these strange creatures and been able to capture it as whales were captured. That never happened. And since the invention of the camera, there have been thousands of pictures taken of whales, sea turtles, sharks, and other sea creatures—but there isn't a single photograph of a "sea serpent."

What, then, did all the people who reported sea serpents actually *see*? Many scientists think they probably saw ordinary things and mistook them for something unusual. A group of dolphins leaping in and out of the water one after another can look like a long, snaky body coiling in and out of the water. A distant clump of floating seaweed can look like a big, swimming animal.

But there are some scientists who say that people such as the two British scientists and the captain of the *Daedalus* could not have been mistaken—they were too experienced. These scientists believe that many of the people who claim to have seen strange animals really did see some kind of unknown creature.

What could this creature be? Some of the scientists think it could be a giant eel. Others think it could be some kind of unknown seal or whale.

So, the age-old mystery of the sea serpent is still unsolved. While most people today do not believe there is any such thing, there are still those who believe there is.

The Mystery of the *Mary Celeste*

As well as being mysterious, the sea is also dangerous. Every year for thousands of years, ships have sailed away never to be seen again. Everyone knew these ships had probably encountered a storm, run onto a reef, or hit an iceberg, and then sunk. Such accidents have always been common dangers of the sea.

But sometimes there would be a mystery about a ship that never got to where it was going. Sometimes, one of these ships would be found weeks, months, or even years later, drifting aimlessly. Some ships have been found with the crew mysteriously dead. Other ships have been found abandoned. People could only wonder about what might have happened.

The most famous of all such mystery ships is the *Mary Celeste*, built in 1861. It was the kind of ship known as a brigantine, which is a small ship with two masts that have different kinds of sails. It belonged to a company that used it for carrying trade goods from one country to another. On November 7, 1872, the *Mary Celeste* sailed from New York, bound for Genoa, Italy, with a cargo of 1,700 barrels of industrial alcohol. Aboard were the

captain, Benjamin Briggs, his wife, their two-year-old daughter, and a crew of seven.

By chance, a ship named the *Dei Gratia* had been docked near the *Mary Celeste.* Her captain and Captain Briggs were old friends. The *Dei Gratia* was going to Europe on the same course as the *Mary Celeste*, and it set sail on November 15. Sea voyages took a long time in those days, and by December 5 the *Dei Gratia* was still several days away from the coast of Europe. That afternoon, its crew sighted another ship in the distance—a ship that was veering to and fro as if no one were steering it. It seemed to be in trouble.

The *Dei Gratia*'s captain took his ship toward the other to see if it needed help. Suddenly, he realized that the ship was the *Mary Celeste.* There was no one at the wheel steering her, and he could not see anyone on deck.

An officer and two sailors rowed over from the *Dei Gratia* to the *Mary Celeste* and went aboard. They searched the ship and found no one. Captain Briggs, his wife and daughter, and the seven crewmen were gone. So was the only lifeboat. But in the crew's quarters were the boots, raincoats, pipes and tobacco, and spare clothing of the *Mary Celeste*'s sailors. And in the captain's cabin were clothing and possessions of the captain and his wife.

It was clear that all the people on the *Mary Celeste* had gotten into the lifeboat and rowed away in a tremendous hurry, leaving everything behind except the clothes they were wearing. But why? Everything seemed to be in good order on the *Mary Celeste*. There was plenty of food and water.

There were no leaks. There was no sign of fire. Why had everyone been in such a desperate rush to get away from the ship?

This question is a mystery that has puzzled people for over a hundred years. Many people tried to figure out the answer—and some of their ideas were strange indeed!

Some people thought that perhaps the *Mary Celeste* had been haunted, and the captain and crew

had left in order to get away from the ghost! Others thought that a sea monster had begun to prey on the people aboard the *Mary Celeste*. And there were those who believed that everyone aboard the ship had been kidnapped by creatures from space!

There were many other ideas as well, although most weren't that fantastic. Many people thought that someone might have killed everyone on the

Mary Celeste and thrown their bodies overboard. However, experts who examined the ship didn't find any sign of a struggle or any trace of blood.

There is one explanation for the *Mary Celeste* mystery that most people now think is probably the right one. It is this:

The *Mary Celeste* went from very cold winter weather in New York to much warmer weather as it neared southern Europe. This could have caused the barrels of alcohol to begin to leak vapor, which would have looked like smoke. Everyone on the ship would have thought there was a fire, and would have expected the alcohol to explode at any moment. They would have hurried to get off the ship before this happened, not taking any time to go for spare clothing or even extra food or water.

The sailors probably rowed as hard as they could in order to get far away from the *Mary Celeste* before it exploded. Soon, there would have been no chance to get back to the ship even had they wanted to. They must have started out to try to row to the nearest land. With luck, they could have made it. But chances are they ran into a storm. The little lifeboat was probably swamped by high waves and the ten people from the *Mary Celeste* drowned.

Something like that is almost certainly what really happened. However, we will never know for sure, and so, for some people, the mystery of the *Mary Celeste* will never truly be solved.

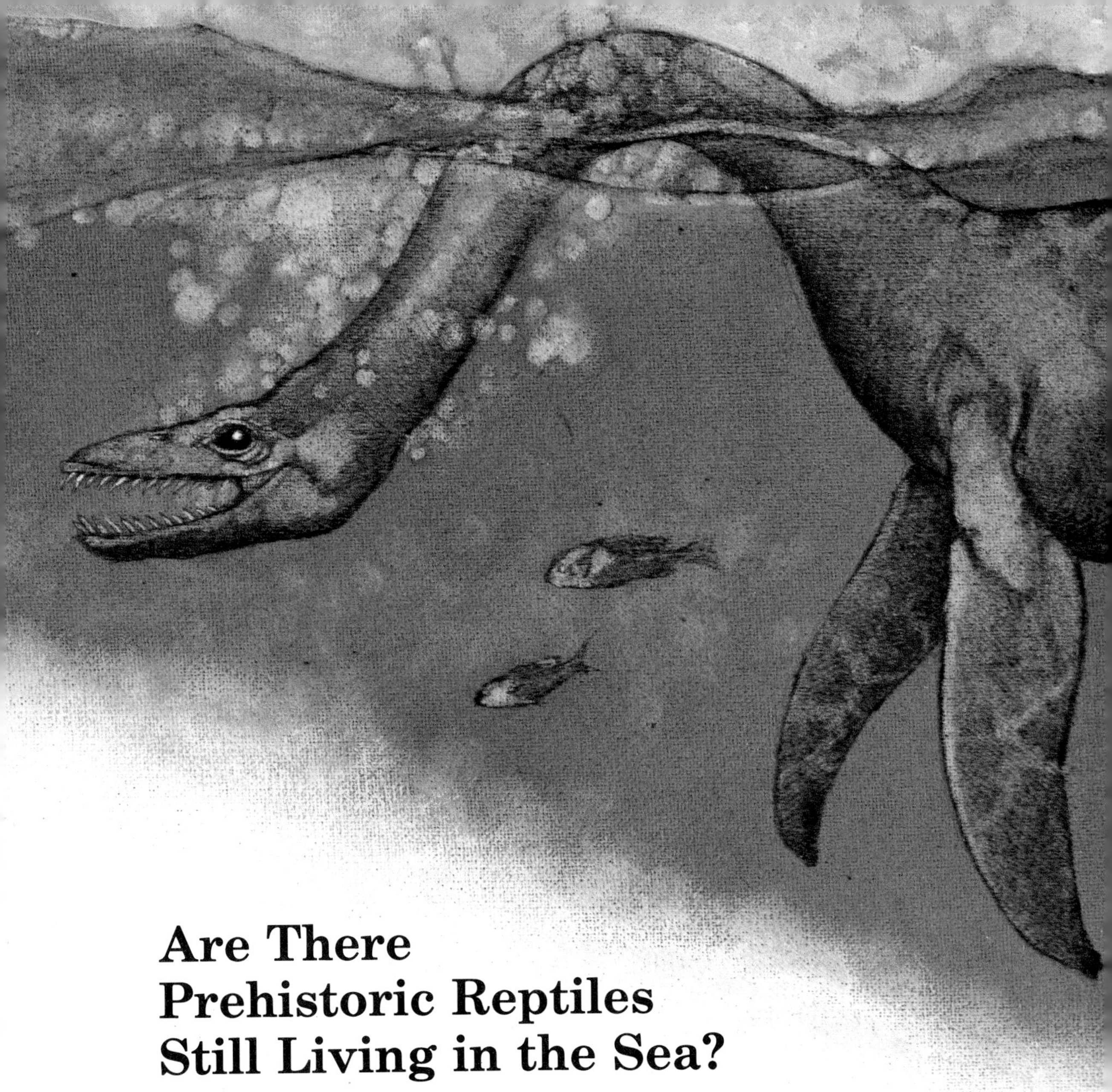

Are There Prehistoric Reptiles Still Living in the Sea?

On April 25, 1977, the Japanese fishing ship *Zuiyo Maru* was dragging its net through waters in the Pacific Ocean near New Zealand. When the net was hauled up, the ship's crewmen saw that instead of a mass of wiggling, flopping fish, it contained the dead, rotting body of some enormous sea animal.

"It's a rotten whale," reported Michihiko Yano, the assistant production manager of the company that owned the ship. "What shall we do?"

"Pull it up as it is," answered the ship's captain. The crew would have to remove the carcass from the net and drop it back into the ocean.

The net was hauled out of the water. Crewmen managed to get ropes around the big body and got it untangled from the net. It was so badly decayed that no one could tell what kind of animal it was.

"That's no whale," said one of the crewmen. "It might be a big seal, though."

"I think it's a turtle," said another. "It's so badly rotted that the shell has come off."

But Michihiko Yano felt there was something strange and unfamiliar about the huge creature. Despite the dreadful smell of its rotting flesh, he carefully measured it. Its head was almost eighteen inches (45 centimeters) long, and it had a neck five feet (1.5 meters) long. The body, from the head to the base of the tail, was nearly twenty feet (6 m) in length. Yano took some photographs of the creature. He also cut off some pieces of one of its fins, which he preserved. Then the strange-looking carcass was dumped back into the sea.

When Yano returned to Japan, he had the photographs developed. Some of Japan's top scientists got together to look at them and try to figure out what the creature might have been.

Some people think this dead sea animal, pulled up by Japanese fishermen in 1977, was a prehistoric plesiosaur.

But they simply couldn't tell. It might have been a big seal, but the tail seemed much too long. It might have been a turtle or other reptile, but didn't seem to have enough bones around the neck for that. It might have been a big basking shark, but the neck seemed too long, the spine too large, and the head much too small. Besides, the creature did not appear to have a fin on its back, as sharks do. Also, it seemed to have four big fins on its underside, while a shark has only two.

From the photographs, it looked as if the creature had been an animal with a small head on a long neck, a big body with four swim fins, and a short tail.

"It must be either a mammal or a reptile," said Professor Ikuo Obata of Japan's National Science

Museum. "But there are too many points that don't fit the mammal theory. To my knowledge, it looks like a plesiosaur."

If the mysterious creature *were* a plesiosaur (PLEE see uh sawr), this would be one of the most fantastic discoveries in history. For plesiosaurs were prehistoric animals—giant sea-dwelling reptiles that lived at the same time as the

dinosaurs. They had small heads, long necks, big bodies with four swim fins, and short tails. It is believed that they all died out about seventy million years ago. So, if the creature the *Zuiyu Maru* had picked up in its net were a plesiosaur, it meant that some of these giant reptiles from the age of the dinosaurs were still living in the Pacific Ocean.

Although this looks like a long-necked prehistoric creature, it is really a dead basking shark that has washed ashore.

A few other scientists agreed with Professor Obata that the creature in the photographs did seem to resemble a plesiosaur much more than a shark. And it really wouldn't be impossible for a certain kind of sea creature to have survived in the ocean for seventy million years—some kinds have survived even longer than that. But most scientists simply didn't think the creature could have been a plesiosaur, and there are good reasons why it might not have been.

For one thing, ships of Japan and other nations have been sailing for more than two hundred years in the part of the Pacific where the creature was found. If there were plesiosaurs living there it seems as if they would surely have been seen long before this. They couldn't have simply been lurking out of sight underwater, because plesiosaurs were air-breathers that swam up at the top of the water. Other air-breathing sea creatures such as whales, sea turtles, and seals, are often seen, and their dead bodies are often washed ashore. This would certainly be true of such large creatures as plesiosaurs, too.

Furthermore, marine biologists—scientists who study the living things of the sea—know that people have often found carcasses of "sea monsters." But these have always turned out to be dead basking sharks. Basking sharks are huge. When the body rots, the lower jaw usually falls off, making the creature look like a strange, long-necked "monster." And a dead whale half-eaten by sharks might look like an unknown monster to some people.

A biochemist at Tokyo University, Dr. Shigeru Kimura, tested the bits of fin that Michihiko Yano had cut off the creature. He found that the fin contained a chemical that, among fish, is found only in the bodies of sharks and rays. So the creature was not a mammal, such as a whale or dolphin. It might have been a reptile, but it was probably a shark.

So, at this time, no one knows what the creature taken out of the waters near New Zealand really was. Only by examining its skeleton would scientists have known for certain. Most scientists think it was probably a shark. But a few still think it might have been a plesiosaur. If so, those prehistoric reptiles, which are supposed to have been extinct for seventy million years, may still be swimming in the Pacific Ocean!

BERMUDA
FLORIDA
The Bermuda Triangle
BAHAMAS
CUBA
PUERTO RICO
DOMINICAN REPUBLIC

Is There Really a Bermuda Triangle Mystery?

Ships and airplanes mysteriously vanishing . . . drifting ships with not a living soul on board . . . reports of "strange-looking" skies and seas. . . . These are the tales that make up the legend of the Bermuda Triangle.

The Bermuda Triangle, also called the Devil's Triangle and the Triangle of Death, lies in the Atlantic Ocean, off the coast of Florida. A line drawn from Florida to the island of Bermuda, from Bermuda down to the island of Puerto Rico, and from Puerto Rico back to Florida, forms a triangle. According to legend, ships sailing into this triangle or airplanes flying through the sky above it are in deadly peril. People say that something causes ships and planes to vanish forever when they go into this area!

The legend of the Bermuda Triangle goes back more than two hundred years. In 1781, a ship of the United States Navy sailed into the Triangle and was never seen again. During the next thirty years, three more U.S. Navy ships also disappeared inside the Triangle.

In 1840, according to legend, a French ship, the *Rosalie*, drifted out of the Triangle in perfect condition—but without a living person aboard. Supposedly, a Swedish ship vanished in the Triangle in 1866, and a Spanish one in 1868. In 1880, a ship of the British Navy, with three hundred naval cadets on board, sailed out of Bermuda into the Triangle and was never seen again. Dozens of search ships sailed into the area to look for some trace of the missing vessel, but they found nothing.

Between 1880 and 1940, dozens of other ships were reported to have vanished in the Triangle, and several others drifted out without a soul on board. Then, as more and more airplanes began to fly over the area, some of them, too, began to vanish!

In 1945, a flight of five U.S. Navy planes took off from Fort Lauderdale, Florida, and flew out over the Triangle. According to the story, the commander of the flight soon radioed back that he and his men were lost. He said that everything looked "wrong" and "strange," and that even the ocean didn't look right! After a time, the radio calls grew weaker and finally stopped. The five planes had disappeared. When other planes went out to search for them, one of those planes vanished as well! Six airplanes had disappeared without a trace!

In 1947, an American Superfortress bomber vanished over the Triangle, and in 1948 a British airliner disappeared. In the years that followed, the

Bermuda Triangle apparently swallowed up many other planes and ships.

To most people, the disappearance of so many ships and planes in one tiny part of the Atlantic Ocean was a tremendous mystery. It seemed as if something inside the Triangle suddenly caught ships and planes unaware, and either caused them to sink or crash or simply swallowed them up.

Could eruptions of an underwater volcano have caused whirlpools that sucked down the ships? Could such eruptions have produced bursts of gas that knocked the planes out of the sky? Did freak storms suddenly catch ships and planes by

surprise? Did some kind of strange "hole" in the area pull in ships and planes and carry them into another universe—or into the past or the future?

The Bermuda Triangle mystery had a great many people concerned during the 1950's and 1960's. It became the subject of many books, movies, and television plays. Then, some people went to work to try to find out exactly what was going on. They discovered some very surprising things.

For one, it turned out that many of the ships reported as vanishing in the Triangle hadn't been anywhere near the Triangle. Most of them had

apparently gone down in storms, thousands of miles away. Writers and reporters had just added them to the Bermuda Triangle mystery to make it more interesting!

What about ships and planes that really had disappeared in the Triangle? People found that many of them, reported as vanishing in good weather for no reason at all, had actually been caught in storms. And there is nothing mysterious about a ship or plane disappearing during a storm at sea.

The investigators also found that many of the stories of mysterious happenings in the Triangle had been made up! For example, the commander of the flight of U.S. Navy planes that vanished never said that everything looked "wrong" and "strange." He reported his compass as not working, and feared he had led the flight off course. Some writers changed his words to make what happened seem strange and fantastic.

So, in other words, a great deal of the Bermuda Triangle mystery and legend is simply made up—it never happened. While a good many ships and planes have disappeared inside the Triangle, no more have disappeared there than in any other part of the ocean. And we know most of the reasons for the disappearances—there is no mystery about them. For example, we know that the five U.S. Navy planes simply flew off course, ran out of gas, and had to come down in the ocean at night. Sadly, the pilots drowned and the planes sank. It was a tragedy, but no mystery.

Today, hardly anyone talks about the Bermuda Triangle mystery. Many young people have never even heard of it. It is all but forgotten because people learned that it was really no mystery at all.

The Real Kraken

An ancient Norse legend tells that down in the deepest, darkest, coldest water of the ocean there dwell enormous octopuslike monsters known as krakens (KRAH kuhnz or KRAY kuhnz). According to legend, a kraken has a body that is a mile-and-a-half (2.4 kilometers) around, with eight long snakelike arms, each as thick as a big tree trunk. Its eyes are fiery red, and as wide as the length of a tall man's body. At times, it is said, one of these creatures may rise to the surface of the sea—and woe betide any ship it might encounter!

The kraken could wrap its arms around a ship and crush it to splinters!

For many hundreds of years, people in some parts of Europe believed such creatures really existed. Books printed in England in 1656 and 1755 talked about krakens as if they were real and quite common. However, as time went on and more and more was learned about the world, most people began to doubt there was such a thing as a kraken. No kraken was ever seen, and no ships were ever attacked. Scientists felt that krakens, like most legendary monsters, were simply made up.

But then, krakenlike creatures began to appear!

In 1853, the body of a huge squid washed up onto a beach in Denmark. A squid is an animal very much like an octopus, except that it has a long pointed body with two fins at the end, and ten arms instead of eight. Ordinary squids, which are plentiful in the ocean, are generally less than a foot (30.5 centimeters) long, but this squid was many times that size. Fishermen cut it up to use for fish bait, and the chunks filled a whole cart. All that was left of it, its parrotlike beak, they gave to a Danish scientist. He found that the beak was many times larger than that of an ordinary squid.

In 1861, a French warship actually fought a battle with a giant squid. The French sailors wounded it with gunshots and captured it. But when they tried to hoist it aboard ship, the body broke apart. They estimated the length of the body to be about eighteen feet (5.5 meters).

During the years since then, a great many other giant squids have been seen, caught, or washed up dead on beaches. The largest one ever measured had a body twenty feet (6.1 m) long and arms thirty-five feet (10.7 m) long, making its total length about fifty-five feet (16.8 m). It was longer than many big dinosaurs.

So, people now realize that the ancient legend of the kraken is based on fact. There really are giant, many-armed creatures living in the deep parts of the ocean.

However, big as these creatures may be, they certainly aren't nearly as big as the old tales said they were. But some people think we haven't encountered any of the *biggest* giant squids. They think there is good evidence that some really enormous giant squids, and perhaps octopuses, too, exist in the sea.

Most of this evidence comes from whales. Some kinds of whales hunt and feed on giant squids. They apparently often have battles with squids in the ocean depths. Squids have many suckers on their snaky arms. These are like rubbery suction cups. Many whales have been found with what seem to be scars made by squid suckers. Some of these marks were so big that it seems they could only have been made by gigantic squids. Many whales have also been found with what seem to be pieces of enormous squid arms in their stomachs. Some of these pieces are reported to be as much as two feet (0.6 m) wide.

However, most scientists don't think this "evidence" is very strong. It seems most likely that the scars found on the bodies of whales are actually marks left by a fish called a lamprey. This fish is a bloodsucker, with a mouth like a suction cup. As for the chunks of huge arms, no scientist has ever seen any such chunk. The stories, then, may simply be exaggerations.

Some people still like to think there may be monstrous krakens deep in the sea. But most scientists think that the giant squids we have found are probably about as big as giant squids get. And for the people who have encountered these creatures—and sometimes even had to battle them—that's plenty big enough!

Mysteries of the Sky

What Are UFO's?

On a June day in 1947, a man named Kenneth Arnold was flying his small airplane over some mountains in the state of Washington. Suddenly, he was startled by a bright flash of light in the sky. He peered about, trying to see what had caused it. After a moment, he caught sight of something—something very strange!

Off to his right, about twenty-three miles (36.8 kilometers) away, he saw nine shiny objects flying in a row. They were moving at a speed of about

1,600 miles (2,570 km) per hour—almost three times as fast as any airplane could then fly! Mr. Arnold later said that the objects didn't fly smoothly, like an airplane, but moved jerkily, like a saucer that someone had sent skipping across water. As he watched them, they rapidly vanished from sight.

Kenneth Arnold talked about what he had seen. His story appeared in newspapers and was discussed on news broadcasts. It interested and excited many people. They wondered what the mysterious flying objects could have been.

This was the beginning of the greatest mystery of our time—the mystery of UFO's, or

Unidentified Flying Objects. For right after Kenneth Arnold saw the strange flying things, many other people began seeing similar unknown flying objects in the sky.

An Air Force pilot flying over Nevada saw a formation of six disk-shaped (circle-shaped) things. The pilot and copilot of an airliner flying over Idaho saw nine disks. One night in Portland, Oregon, policemen and dozens of other people saw groups of strange objects in the sky. In Arizona, a man took two pictures of a fast-flying object that seemed to be shaped like the heel of a man's shoe!

All these stories, and others, were printed in newspapers and reported on radio and television. Across the United States, many people were curious and excited—and some were worried and fearful! What were these mysterious things that had suddenly begun appearing in the sky? They certainly weren't airplanes.

There were lots of different ideas. Many people believed all the stories were simply made up. Others thought that perhaps the people who said they had seen UFO's were just mistaken about what they had seen. Some people thought the objects were a new, secret kind of aircraft. And some thought they were spaceships from another planet!

By the beginning of 1948, so many reports of UFO's had been made that the United States Air

In 1948 and 1949, hundreds of people claimed to have seen many different kinds of UFO's.

Force became concerned. It is the job of the U.S. Air Force to protect the nation from an attack from the sky. If UFO's were real, they might be dangerous. What if they were secret weapons belonging to an unfriendly country? The Air Force began to investigate.

During 1948, reports of UFO's continued to pour in. In Canada, a number of objects flying at the incredible speed of 9,000 miles (14,484 km) per hour were tracked on radar. An airline pilot and copilot saw a huge, cigar-shaped object with what looked like a row of windows running along its side. A U.S. Air Force pilot in a fighter plane chased an oval-shaped object for ten minutes. UFO's were seen over Japan and Germany, as well as the United States and Canada.

By now, people everywhere had heard of UFO's, or "flying saucers" as they were often called. Stories about them filled the newspapers almost every day. There were articles about them in magazines and special programs about them on radio and television. And people learned that UFO's were *not* something new—they had been seen before!

During World War II, many Army and Navy pilots had seen disks and glowing lights in the sky. Such things had also been seen off and on throughout the 1930's and 1920's. And back in 1897—long before there were *any* airplanes or airships in the United States—thousands of people across the country had seen strange, glowing, cigar-shaped objects in the sky!

During 1948 and 1949, hundreds of people reported seeing objects that looked like metal disks, cigar-shaped rockets, or glowing balls of light. These things flew around airplanes, flew over towns and cities, and circled and hovered near secret military bases. They were seen almost everywhere in the world.

A scientist hired by the Air Force examined most of the reports and talked to the people who had made them. Experts carefully examined all the

This glowing light was photographed in the sky above Minnesota in 1965.

This object was photographed over Oregon in 1950.

This object was photographed over Brazil in 1958.

pictures that had been taken of UFO's. By the end of 1949, the Air Force announced that all the reports of UFO's were either mistakes or hoaxes (made-up). And all the pictures were either fakes or pictures of ordinary things. As far as the Air Force was concerned, there were really no such things as UFO's.

But a great many people simply did not believe this. Of course, there *were* some tricksters and pretenders who had made up stories of UFO's. There were also many people who had just made

This glowing, moving light appeared over New Mexico in 1957.

silly mistakes. But many of the people who had seen UFO's were police officers, scientists, Air Force and airline pilots, and public officials. These were educated, intelligent people who were not likely to make silly mistakes or to make up stories for fun or to draw attention to themselves. Many Americans believed that such people really had seen UFO's when they said they did, and that UFO's really existed. They wondered if the Air Force was "covering up," pretending that UFO's weren't real!

However, the Air Force continued to investigate UFO reports, and reports continued to pour in. It seemed as if there were suddenly more UFO's than ever! In 1952, the Air Force received more than 1,500 reports, and there were many more that were not even sent in.

In July 1952, night after night, clusters of glowing lights were seen over Washington, D.C. Radar screens on the ground seemed to show that the lights were solid objects. Air Force pilots, sent up to investigate, saw the lights zipping past their planes. One pilot was badly frightened when his plane seemed to be surrounded for a time by a large number of the glowing UFO's.

In August and September there were strange, frightening reports of UFO's that had apparently come down and landed. One report even described an encounter with a "creature" from a UFO!

The first report, in August, came from near Palm Beach, Florida. A Scoutmaster was driving three of his Boy Scouts home from an outing when they all saw a cluster of blurry lights sail down out of the sky into a nearby patch of woods. Thinking an airplane might have crashed, the Scoutmaster stopped the car and went by himself, on foot, toward where they had last seen the lights.

The man claimed that he reached a clearing and saw a huge dome-shaped craft hovering silently over the ground. Suddenly, what seemed to be a red ball of fire shot toward him from the craft and he fell unconscious. When Air Force investigators questioned the three boys, they all said they had not seen any dome-shaped craft, but they did see flashes of red light shoot toward their Scoutmaster and knock him down. Later, when investigators

examined the place where the dome-shaped craft was supposed to have hovered, they found that the roots of all the grass in a broad circle were scorched—but not the top of the grass.

The second report, in September, came from the tiny town of Flatwoods, West Virginia. A group of teen-aged and younger boys saw what they thought was a meteor fall out of the sky and land on a nearby wooded hill. Two of the boys went to get their mother, and she went with all the boys to look for the object.

The woman and the six youngsters later claimed that they found a big, glowing, fiery red shape resting on the hill. A strange, sickening odor hung over the area. As the people stared, they suddenly saw a creature with a bright red face and glowing green eyes floating toward the red shape. The creature wore a kind of robe and hood. The woman and boys turned and ran. Later, when a sheriff and some men went to the hill, they noticed the strange odor and found a large, round, mashed-down place in the grass where the glowing red object might have sat.

In October, in France, hundreds of people saw what seemed to be a cluster of glowing globes hovering around a giant cigar-shaped object. In November, in South Carolina, hundreds of people saw what seemed to be a huge metal disk in the sky.

Reports of this sort continued to come in throughout the 1950's. They came from all over the world. The air forces of several other countries besides the United States were now investigating UFO's, but no one had yet been able to find out anything about them.

A great many people still thought UFO's were space vehicles from somewhere. Some people thought they were "time travelers" from the future. Some believed they were angels—or devils! Many scientists thought UFO's were just ordinary things, such as meteors, reflections of light, and so on, that had been mistaken for something else. And some scientists and other people thought that those who told of UFO's had either imagined what they told—or made it up!

Stories of UFO's continued all through the 1960's. Some of these tales were weird and frightening. A number of people told of being kidnapped by strange creatures who took them onto UFO's and examined them. Other people suffered odd burns and injuries which they claimed had been caused by UFO's.

All this time, year after year since 1949, the United States Air Force had investigated reports. By 1969, the reports totaled 12,618. That year, the Air Force announced that the UFO's in 11,917 of the reports had turned out to be either just ordinary things that people had mistaken for something else, or hoaxes. The Air Force admitted that 701 of the reports really couldn't be explained. But despite this, the Air Force said that it did not believe there was any such thing as a UFO and it would not investigate any more reports of them.

A great many people in the United States believed that the Air Force itself was guilty of a hoax! These people insisted that the Air Force had really found out what UFO's were, but was hiding the truth from everyone. Some of these people formed organizations to keep the investigation of UFO's going.

Toward the end of the 1970's, it seemed as if there were fewer reports of UFO's. But what really happened was that newspapers and radio and TV news programs just weren't reporting them as often. Sometimes the reports given to newspapers weren't even printed, because it was felt that people weren't as interested in UFO's as they had been.

However, people were still seeing many UFO's. In 1981, there were more than two thousand reports from all over the world. Disk-shaped objects and other UFO's are still being reported, and many people claim to have encountered strange creatures that have come out of UFO's.

What are all these strange objects people have seen in the sky? What made the round, flat, burned places on the ground where people claim that UFO's had landed? What caused the burns and injuries to people who said they had been harmed by UFO's? What really happened to all the people who claim to have been kidnapped by UFO creatures?

Many scientists think there never really were any UFO's. They think that many people saw

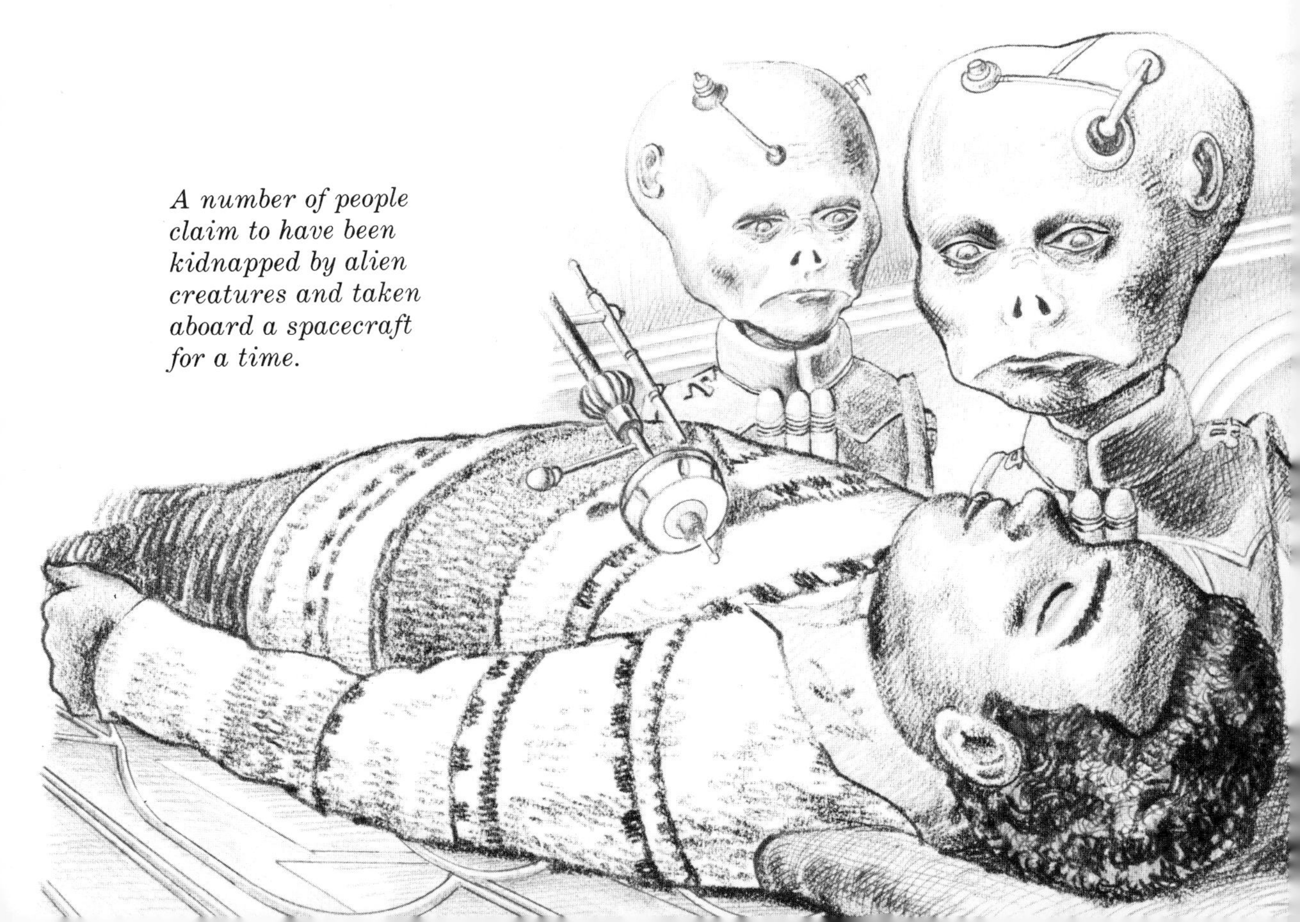

A number of people claim to have been kidnapped by alien creatures and taken aboard a spacecraft for a time.

At certain times, the planet Venus (above) *shown here at dusk, is brighter than any star in the sky. Many people have thought that this brilliant light was a UFO. Ball lightning* (right) *sometimes looks like a solid, hovering ball that people have thought was a UFO.*

ordinary things in the sky and mistook them for something else. For example, people have reported the planet Venus as a UFO. At times, Venus, which looks like a star, is so bright that it can even be seen in the daytime. Many people seeing a bright light hanging in the sky thought they saw a UFO.

Ball lightning was another thing many people probably saw and reported as a UFO. Ball lightning is one form of lightning. It appears as a glowing, fiery ball that floats for several seconds before it disappears. It may be red, yellow, or orange, and is usually about the size of a grapefruit. In daylight it often looks silvery, like metal. It often seems to hover in one place, as many UFO's were said to do. And it often vanishes suddenly, as many UFO's did. It can suddenly drop down to the ground, and where it touches, it can leave a broad, round, slightly burnt spot.

Many other things could also be mistaken for UFO's. A weather balloon looks like a huge silvery disk racing across the sky. A meteor may look like a bright, blazing ball traveling at enormous speed. Lights on the ground, such as automobile headlights, are sometimes reflected into the sky, where they look like glowing, moving spots. Many scientists think that such things as these caused most UFO reports.

However, a number of scientists and other people do not think all the UFO reports can be explained this way. They feel there is good evidence that some UFO's really were different and unusual. Many of these scientists think UFO's actually could be some kind of craft from somewhere. Most of them think UFO's should be carefully investigated with the best scientific methods.

So, while for some people the UFO mystery is solved, because they don't think there ever were any, for others it is still going on. People still report seeing UFO's, and will probably continue to see them. Perhaps someday we'll be able to find out for sure whether UFO's are all just imagination, whether they are caused by such things as ball lightning or reflections, or whether they are actually something strange and wonderful.

What Made the Mystery Cloud?

Just before midnight on April 9, 1984, a Japan Air Lines cargo plane was heading across the Pacific Ocean between Tokyo, Japan, and Anchorage, Alaska. Suddenly, the pilot saw a shocking, startling sight. Ahead, a gigantic mushroom-shaped cloud was rising into the sky!

As far as the pilot knew, only one thing could cause such a cloud—an atomic explosion! He believed that, for some reason, a Russian atomic missile had been exploded in the ocean. He swerved to fly around the cloud, for to fly through it could have meant certain death from atomic radiation for himself and all the plane's crew!

But as it turned out, the cloud had not been caused by an atomic explosion. Instruments in Japan and on nearby Pacific islands would have detected any atomic explosion—but the instruments hadn't shown a thing. And when a Japanese Air Self-Defense Force plane brought in a sample of dust from the cloud for testing, the tests showed there was no atomic radiation in the cloud. Obviously, there hadn't been an atomic explosion.

The only other thing that scientists knew could cause such a cloud was the eruption of a volcano. Sure enough, when scientists checked they found that a volcano known as Kaitoku Seamount had erupted on the day the cloud was seen.

However, Kaitoku Seamount is nine hundred miles (1,448 kilometers) from where the giant cloud was seen. And when scientists did more checking, they found that when the volcano erupted, the wind had been blowing in the opposite direction from where the mushroom cloud had risen. Thus, smoke and dust from the Kaitoku

An atomic explosion causes a huge, mushroom-shaped cloud. Such a cloud was seen over the Pacific Ocean in 1984. But no atomic explosion had taken place.

eruption couldn't have formed the cloud. That smoke and dust had been blown the other way.

So the gigantic mushroom cloud seen on that April morning was not caused by either an atomic explosion or a volcanic eruption. Yet, scientists say those are the only things that could cause such a cloud. If neither thing happened, then what made the cloud?

To this date, no one has the slightest idea.

What Fell from the Sky in 1908?

On June 30, 1908, a fiery ball as bright as the sun came streaking down out of the sky over Siberia, which is the eastern half of Russia. It moved with a sound like a steady roar of thunder that made houses shake. Then it struck the earth with a tremendous explosion that sent a burst of fire shooting into the air, followed by a rolling cloud of smoke. The explosion was so powerful that all across Europe and Asia, seismographs—machines that measure the force of an earthquake—showed that a tremendous earthquake had taken place in Siberia.

However, this object from the sky came down in a wild, remote part of Siberia, a great many miles (kilometers) from the nearest town or village. It wasn't until thirteen years later that Leonid Kulik, a Russian scientist visiting in Siberia, heard about it from people who had seen the fiery ball and heard the explosion. And it wasn't until six years after *that* that the scientist was able to put together an expedition to try to find out what had happened. He believed that the object must have been a huge meteorite, and he hoped to find the remains of it.

A meteorite is a chunk of rock and metal that has fallen to Earth from space. Millions of such chunks, of all sizes, circle around the sun just as Earth and the other planets do. Often, one of them comes close enough for Earth's gravity to seize it. The gravity pulls the chunk—which is called a meteoroid when it is out in space—down into Earth's atmosphere. The meteoroid travels at such tremendous speed that when it enters Earth's atmosphere and moves through air, it heats up and begins to burn. The burning meteoroid is called a meteor, and any part of it that reaches the ground without burning up is called a meteorite. Often, when a large meteorite hits the ground, it makes a deep pit called a crater.

The Russian scientist, Leonid Kulik, expected to find a gigantic crater, perhaps with some remains of the meteorite at the bottom. But when he and the others on the expedition reached the place where the object from space had apparently come down, they were surprised. What they found were thousands of tree trunks lying in a huge circle, all their leaves and branches burnt away. It was easy to see that a tremendous explosion had flung the

The object from space that came down in Siberia in 1908 hurled thousands of trees in a great circle.

trees about this way—but there was absolutely no trace of what had caused the explosion! No crater and no remains of a meteorite could be seen.

This was a mystery. What could have caused such a great explosion without leaving a trace of itself? Scientists and other people have tried to figure this out for more than half a century!

A few people believe that what came out of the sky and exploded on that day in 1908 was nothing less than a spaceship from another world! They think the ship was powered by a nuclear engine that blew up. The atomic explosion turned the ship into a cloud of vapor that spread out and left no trace. But scientists don't think this is what really happened.

A few scientists have suggested that Earth ran into a small black hole. A black hole is a huge star that has collapsed into a small, invisible object with tremendous gravity. But most scientists don't think the object that exploded over the Siberian forest could have been a black hole.

Some scientists think that the object was a small comet. A comet isn't solid like a meteorite—it's nothing more than a ball of snow and ice mixed with dust. A comet about one hundred yards (91 meters) wide would mostly burn away as it fell through the atmosphere. This would account for the fiery ball that people saw. Finally, the tightly packed center would explode from heat, turning to

When a meteorite strikes Earth, it usually makes a large hole. This hole, the Great Meteor Crater in Arizona, is about 4,150 feet (1,265 meters) across and 570 feet (174 meters) deep.

steam and dust, and everything would vanish without a trace. This would account for why no crater and no remains were found.

But a number of scientists don't think the object was a comet either. They think a comet would have melted long before it could explode. They think the object was a meteorite after all—a huge meteorite that exploded so violently it was shattered into billions of tiny pieces, most of them too small to be seen.

In recent years, a number of tiny pieces of metal have been found on the ground in that part of Siberia. Scientists who have carefully examined these pieces say they contain the same kinds of metal that are always found in meteorites and that they must have come from a meteorite. So perhaps the mystery of the object that came from space in 1908 has finally been solved. It was probably a gigantic meteorite that exploded into dust before it hit the ground.

What Were the Green Fireballs?

Late in 1948, people in and around Albuquerque, New Mexico, saw bright streaks of green light flashing through the sky. Many people thought these must be meteors. On December 5, the crews of two airplanes flying near Albuquerque saw what they thought were green meteors that flashed past their planes.

All this was most unusual. For so many meteors to come down in the same place would be just about impossible. Furthermore, these "meteors" just

didn't seem to act right. Meteors come slanting down out of the sky at tremendous speed, but these green fireballs seemed to move in almost a straight line, rather slowly. In fact, the crew of one of the airplanes thought that the fireball they had seen actually rose *up* slightly before it passed them—which a falling meteor couldn't possibly do.

At the time, there were several important military bases in that part of New Mexico. On the chance that these strange green fireballs could be dangerous to the bases, the U.S. Air Force began to investigate them. For maybe they weren't meteors—maybe they were some kind of missile that had been fired at the bases from another country! The Air Force called in a scientist who was an expert on meteors and asked him to try to find out if the fireballs really were meteors.

The scientist knew that when falling meteors strike the ground they always leave at least some tiny pieces. All he had to do was find where some fireballs had hit the ground and see if there were any pieces. By talking with many people who had seen the fireballs, he was able to figure out which way the fireballs had gone and where they had come down. This was the same system he always used when searching for meteorite pieces.

However, when the scientist and his assistants searched some of the places where fireballs would have come down, they found absolutely nothing. This made the scientist wonder if the fireballs really had been meteors. If not, what were they?

During the next few years, green fireballs were seen off and on in New Mexico and several other Southwestern States. In 1951, more than 165 people saw a huge green fireball flash through the sky in Arizona. Many of these people said that the fireball moved in a nearly straight line and exploded in the sky. It did not make any noise, either as it was moving or when it exploded. This was very strange, for meteors nearly always move with a loud roaring noise and make loud explosions.

In the years after 1951, green fireballs were seen less and less often. Apparently none have been seen since 1954.

What were these bright green balls of fire? What caused them and why did they stop appearing?

At the time, some scientists believed the fireballs were meteors. These scientists thought that from 1948 to 1954 Earth was moving through a part of space filled with chunks of rock that cause what is called a "meteor shower." When Earth left that part of space, the shower stopped. This is not unusual.

Other scientists didn't think the fireballs could possibly be meteors—they were the wrong color, they moved too slowly and in too straight a line, they didn't make any noise, and they didn't leave any pieces. But what they were if they weren't meteors, no one could say, then or now. The mystery of the green fireballs is still a mystery.

Mysterious Things from Long Ago

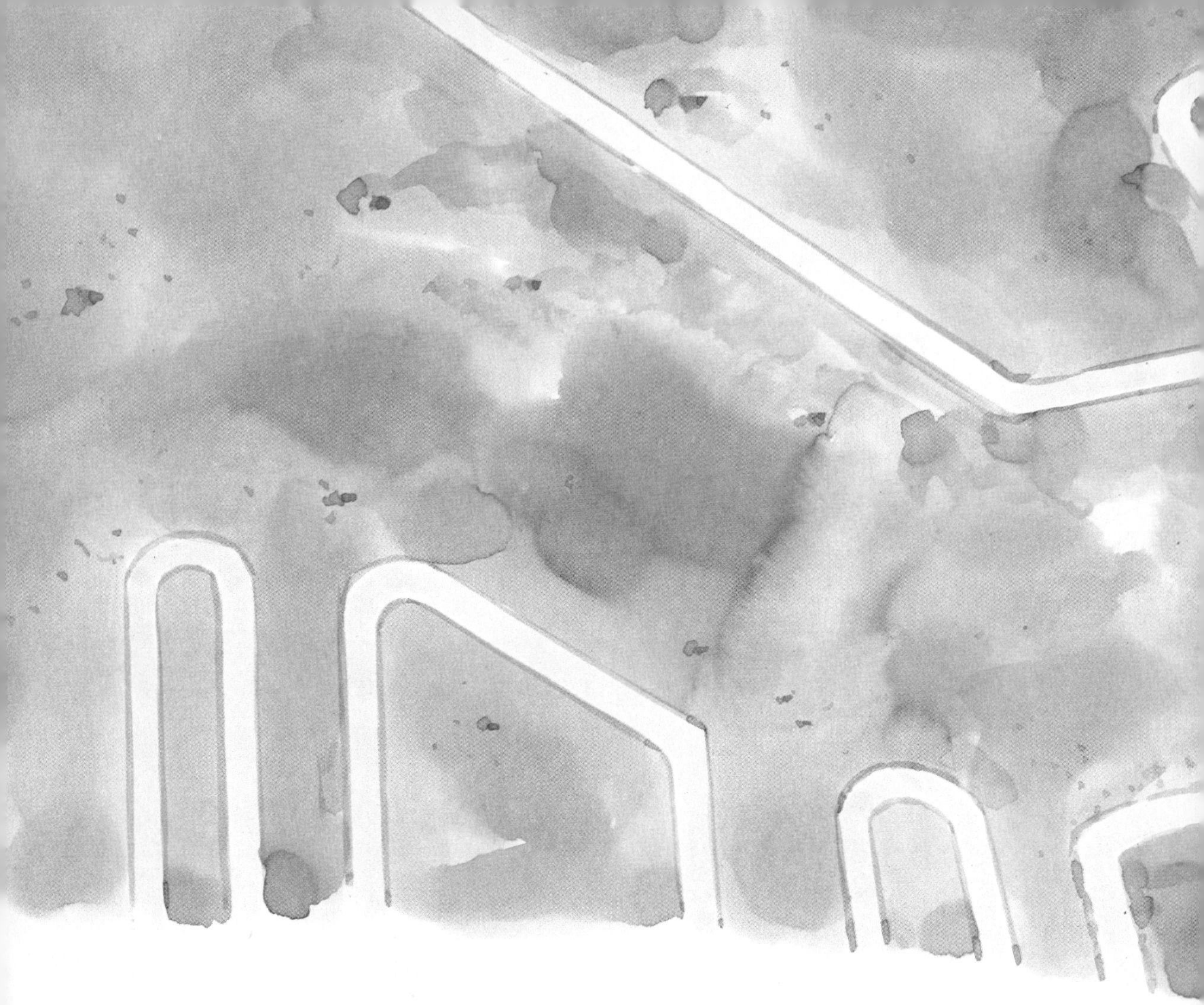

The Mysterious Desert Pictures

Anyone flying over the southern part of Peru in South America can look down and see a strange sight. Far below, on the brown desert near the town of Nazca, there are huge pictures—a running fox, a flying hummingbird, a scurrying spider, and other creatures. These pictures are boxed in and

crisscrossed by many long, straight lines going in all directions. The lines form squares, triangles, and other shapes.

Of course, if these things can be seen from high in the sky, they must be gigantic. And they are. The straight lines are thousands of feet (meters) long. The pictures, which are made of lines, are hundreds of feet long. A person standing on the ground near the lines can see some of them—they stretch out like long, narrow roads. But to see the pictures and the shapes formed by the long lines, you have to be high in the sky.

However, someone made all these pictures and lines long before there were any airplanes or balloons, or any other way for people to get up into the sky to see them! Scientists believe these pictures and lines were made anywhere from five hundred to twenty-five hundred years ago, by the Indian people who then lived in this part of Peru. They were made simply by picking up rocks and sweeping away the brownish topsoil of the desert to show the light pinkish soil beneath. Many people probably worked long hours to make each line and picture.

The mystery is, *why* did those people of long ago work so hard to make these pictures and designs when they couldn't get into the sky to see them? There are a lot of ideas about this.

A few people think that perhaps those Indians of long ago *could* get up into the sky. Perhaps they had invented balloons! But this doesn't seem very likely. For one thing, they didn't have the kinds of materials they would have needed to make balloons.

A few other people—a very few—think the pictures and designs were made to be seen by

This picture of a spider in the desert near Nazca, Peru, can be seen only from high in the sky.

The straight lines made on the desert in Peru are thousands of feet (meters) long. The spirals are hundreds of feet (meters) wide.

people or creatures from space! These people believe that, long ago, astronauts from outer space visited Earth and landed in the part of Peru where the pictures now are. They believe that after the astronauts left, the Indian people made the lines and pictures to show the astronauts where to land if they ever came back.

However, scientists who have carefully examined the lines and pictures don't think that idea is very likely either. They have found that the long straight lines and the pictures were made at different times, probably many hundreds of years apart. Thus, they were probably made for two quite different reasons.

There are other guesses as to why the pictures were made. Perhaps the Indians made them so that a sky god they believed in could look down on them. On the other hand, maybe the pictures weren't made to be looked at. Many scientists think they may have been made for people to walk on. Perhaps people followed the lines as part of some special religious or magical ceremony.

As for the long straight lines, most scientists think these probably form a kind of calendar. Perhaps this is the way the people kept track of the places where the sun, moon, and some of the stars and constellations rose and set on certain days of the year. For, it has been found that a person who stands at one end of a certain line at a certain time of the year will see the sun rise or set exactly at the other end of the line.

The Indians could have used such a calendar to tell them what days to plant certain crops, what days to harvest, and so on. Many people of long ago had such calendars, made of lines of rocks, huge boulders placed at special spots, and other kinds of markings.

So, scientists think they have partly solved the mystery of the long lines and giant pictures. The lines probably formed a calendar and the pictures were probably used for ceremonies. But we may never know for sure.

The Secret of the Great Stone Monuments

Throughout much of the world—in western Europe, northern Africa, the Near East, India, Japan, and parts of Southeast Asia—there stand many strange old monuments formed of enormous stones. Some of these monuments are simply single tall stones, standing all by themselves. Others are rings, rows, and clusters of many huge stones, standing upright. Still others are numbers of huge stones piled together to form a large room.

Some of these monuments are prehistoric. They were made thousands of years ago by people we know almost nothing about. Others are less than a thousand years old. But there are many mysteries connected with all of them. What were they for? Why is it that they are often so much alike, even though they are in places thousands of miles (kilometers) apart? Did people just happen to get the same idea in so many different places, or did the idea for such monuments start in one place and slowly spread out around the world?

Some of the piles of stone form large rooms that are burial places. When, at a later time, scientists opened these tombs, they found them crammed with the bones of hundreds of people.

There are some strange things about these

tombs. For one thing, the bones in all the tombs were broken into small pieces. How did this happen—or why? For another thing, each monument is built so that it lines up in a north-south or east-west direction. Why?

An even bigger mystery is that when people opened other rooms, they found them empty. There were no bones or anything else in them. It must have taken scores of people to pile those huge, heavy stones together to make a big room. After going to all that trouble, why didn't they use the rooms?

While it took scores of people to make the room monuments, it must have taken hundreds of people to make some of the others. One of the best known of these is Stonehenge, in England. Many of its

stones have toppled over and lie on the ground. But when Stonehenge was built, about 3,500 years ago, it was a ring of thirty huge, gray stones, with long, flat stones lying across their tops. Inside this ring were other rings and half-rings, one inside another.

Not far from Stonehenge stand the remains of another strange, ancient monument, known as Avebury. Little is now left of it, but long ago it was a great ring of one hundred huge stones with two smaller rings side by side within it. Two long paths, lined on both sides with rows of big stones, once led to the large ring.

Just across the English Channel, on the coast of France, there are other stone monuments. One of these, near the village of Carnac, is formed of more than three thousand tall, heavy boulders. These stand row upon row, spreading out over nearly two miles (3.2 km). And there are hundreds of other monuments, from small circles to single tall stones, throughout England, Scotland, France, Denmark, and other parts of western Europe.

The people who built these things were much like what are often called "cave people." They lived in huts and wore clothes made from animal skins. They had only simple tools, such as stone hammers, shovels made from the shoulder bones of oxen, and pickaxes made from deer antlers. With such crude tools they dug the huge stones out of the ground and sometimes even cut them into special shapes.

This photograph shows the inside of an ancient stone tomb near Carnac, France.

Stonehenge is an ancient monument in England. No one is certain what it was used for.

These rows of big stones near Carnac, France, were set up thousands of years ago, but no one knows why.

The people who built Stonehenge brought some of the stones from as far as three hundred miles (480 km) away. They dragged other stones—some of which weighed as much as fifty tons (45 metric tons)—more than twenty miles (32 km) from where they were dug to where Stonehenge was built. There they managed to stand each stone on end, exactly where it belonged. They raised other stones up as much as twenty-two feet (6.6 meters) to place them on top of the upright stones. All this

must have been a tremendous job for people with no machinery!

What made those people of long ago work so hard to put up these rings and rows of giant stones? Places such as Stonehenge, Avebury, and Carnac must have been tremendously important to those people. But why? What did they use these places for?

Apparently Stonehenge had something to do with watching, and perhaps worshiping, the sun.

The ancient people made a broad path that leads into Stonehenge. A person standing in the middle of Stonehenge at dawn on the longest day of the year, which is the first day of summer, will see the sun rise exactly at the end of the path. This happens only on that one day. Stonehenge was almost certainly put where it is, and built the way it was, so that this would happen. Was Stonehenge a kind of temple where people gathered at dawn on the first day of summer to worship the rising sun?

Some scientists believe it may have been a great deal more than that. They think it may actually have been what we would now call an observatory—a place for keeping track of the movements of the sun, moon, and stars. They believe they have found that almost every stone lines up with something that happens in the sky on certain days—such as the rising and setting of the sun and moon on the first days of summer and winter, the rising of certain stars on midsummer night, and so on. Some of these scientists believe that almost every other ancient circle, or row, or single standing stone was used in much the same way. Even the monuments that form big rooms may have been used for such a purpose.

If this is true, it means that the people who built those monuments so long ago were far more advanced than most people today think they were. Not only did they know a lot about astronomy, but they also must have known a lot about mathematics.

But why would those ancient people have cared about such things as the first day of summer or winter, or eclipses of the sun or moon, or the rising and setting of stars? Perhaps these were holy things for them—an important part of their religion. Perhaps some of those days were special days when certain things had to be done, such as planting or harvesting particular crops. Perhaps places such as Stonehenge and Carnac were used as a calendar, to keep count of the days in a year.

But we can never really know for sure. None of the people who built any of these stone monuments, anywhere in the world, left any writing to tell us what the monuments were for. There is no way we can guess what went on in the minds of those people who lived so long ago. Their ways of life, their beliefs, and their reasons for doing things have been lost. And so, most of the secrets of the stone monuments will probably be secrets forever.

What Was the *Sirrush* of Babylon?

In 1902, a group of scientists and workmen dug up part of the wall of a 2,500-year-old city. On that wall was a mystery.

The city was Babylon, which once stood on the banks of the Euphrates River in the Near East, in what is now the nation of Iraq. Babylon was once the capital of the kingdom of Babylonia, and one of the world's greatest cities. It was a huge square of houses, temples, and palaces, surrounded by a high wall made of shiny, colored bricks. At several places in the wall there were huge gateways with gigantic gates of bronze.

What the scientists discovered and dug up was a

part of the wall with a gateway. The gateway was decorated with sculptures of three kinds of animals, arranged in rows. One animal was a lion and another was a bull. The third was a strange creature such as none of the scientists had ever seen.

The creature had a scaly body with a long tail and a long snakelike neck. A forked tongue, like the tongue of a snake, stuck out of its mouth, and a long horn stuck up from its forehead. Its front legs looked much like the legs and feet of a cat. But it had scaly back legs, with clawed feet like those of a bird or reptile.

This dragon, or sirrush, *once decorated the main gate of the ancient city of Babylon.*

Thus, it seemed to be a creature made up of parts of several different animals. The artists had shown the muscles and skin and hair of the lion and bull so well that those animals looked almost real. And what they showed of this creature, too, looked almost real. It looked as if it had been copied from a live animal! In fact, Professor Robert Koldeway, the scientist who discovered the wall, said that if it weren't for the difference between the creature's front and back legs, ". . . such an animal might actually have existed."

Surprising though it seems, even though the scientists had never seen this creature before, they knew what it was supposed to be. For the king who had the gate decorated with these animals—the

Babylonian king we know as Nebuchadnezzar (nehb uh kuhd NEHZ uhr)—had left writings that described the decoration. These writings had been found and translated. King Nebuchadnezzar had called the creature a *sirrush*, which was the Babylonian word for—dragon!

There is an ancient story, which can be found in some versions of the Bible, that tells of a live *sirrush*, or dragon, that was kept in a temple in Babylon during the days of King Nebuchadnezzar. This creature was worshiped as a god. According to the story, the Hebrew prophet Daniel proved that the creature was not a god by feeding it poisoned food that killed it.

Because of that story, and because the sculptures look so real, the *sirrush* on the wall of Babylon is a mystery for some people. They wonder why the *sirrush* on the wall is shown with two real animals, as if it, too, were real. They wonder if it is just an imaginary, made-up creature, or if it really *was* copied from a live animal—the dragon that was said to live in the temple during the days of King Nebuchadnezzar.

Could there have been some kind of strange, dragonlike reptile living in the Near East or some nearby African country 2,500 years ago? It seems doubtful, for scientists have never found bones or any other trace of such a creature. But some people will always wonder.

What Do Prehistoric Cave Paintings Mean?

One of the greatest discoveries about prehistoric people was made a little more than a hundred years ago by a nine-year-old girl!

The girl's name was Maria, and she was the daughter of Don Marcelino de Sautuola, a Spanish nobleman. His hobby was searching for the weapons, tools, and remains of the prehistoric people who lived in Europe more than ten thousand years ago. One day in 1879, the Marquis was digging among the stones of a cave known as Altamira, where he had found a few prehistoric objects. With him was Maria.

After a time, the little girl grew bored. Taking up one of the candles her father had brought to light the cave, she wandered into a short tunnel. She happened to glance up at the rock ceiling, which was just slightly above her head. After a moment, her eyes grew wide with surprise.

"Bulls!" she exclaimed. "Bulls! Bulls!"

Her father, thinking she was playing some game with him, crawled into the tunnel, which was too small for him to stand up in. "You see bulls, do you?" he asked, smiling. "Where are they?"

Maria pointed up at the ceiling. "There are lots of bulls," she said excitedly. "They are all red!"

Still smiling, Don Marcelino looked upward. After a moment his eyes, too, widened in astonishment. Painted in red and black on the bumpy rock of the cave ceiling was a row of bulky, horned animals that did, indeed, look like bulls. There were also boars, stags, and other animals. As he stared at these marvelous paintings, he realized that Maria had made a great discovery. He felt certain that these paintings had been made many thousands of years ago by prehistoric people!

The prehistoric paintings in Altamira were the

first such cave paintings discovered. Since that time many others have been found, mostly in caves in France and Spain. The artists had painted in the dark caves, by the light of crude lamps—burning wicks of twisted animal fur, floating in animal fat in clay bowls. For paint they used such things as powdered charcoal and ground red and brown rock, mixed with animal fat.

Sculptures and carvings have been found as well. Some of these paintings and sculptures are as much as thirty thousand years old. Some were made as "recently" as ten thousand years ago. They have been preserved in the caves, where there is no wind, rain, or sunlight to wear them away, for all those thousands of years.

Most of the paintings and sculptures are of prehistoric animals such as woolly mammoths and rhinoceroses, and of bison, horses, and deer. A very few show people. And some are simply designs and shapes that are meaningless to us today. But artists of today agree that most of the prehistoric cave paintings and sculptures are good art. The animals are real-looking, and when shown in action they seem lively. The people who painted the pictures, or who carved or molded the sculptures, were true artists.

But there are some big mysteries about all these prehistoric works of art. For one thing, why were they made?

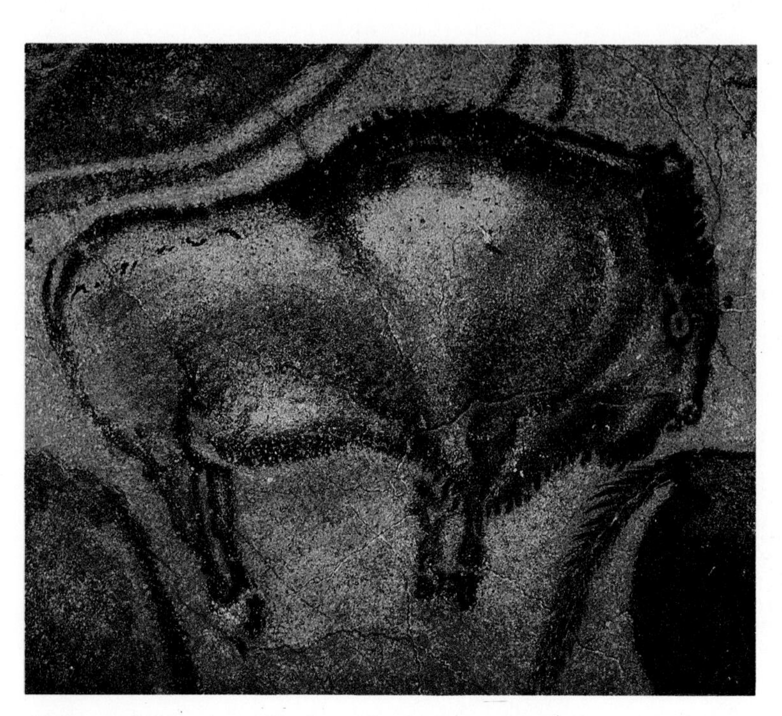

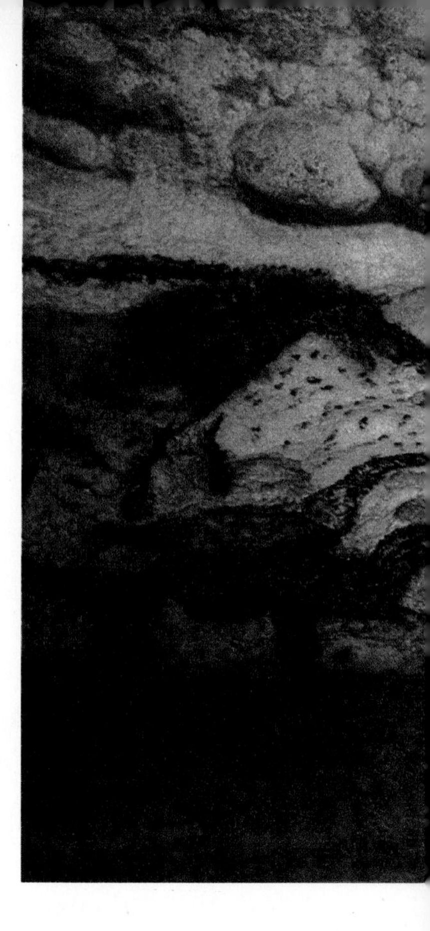

This prehistoric painting of a bull was found on the wall of the cave at Altamira, Spain.

It might seem that prehistoric people made paintings and sculptures for the same reason that we make them today—to look at, and to decorate the places where we live. But that just doesn't seem to be the case. Many of the cave paintings and sculptures are actually hidden away. They are in nooks, crannies, corners, and pits that are very difficult to get into—and impossible to live in.

To see many of these works of art, people would have had to crawl on their stomachs for long distances through narrow, winding tunnels,

These paintings are on the ceiling of the cave at Lascaux, France.

clamber down into pits, and squeeze their way into crevices! It certainly doesn't seem likely that the artists would have made their work so hard to get to if they wanted people to see it.

There are also some strange things about many of the paintings and sculptures themselves. They are chipped and scarred, as if they might have been stabbed with a sharp point. Some of them have pointed, v-shaped marks painted around them. Some are covered with red spots. What can these scars and marks and dots mean?

Some scientists think the prehistoric people used the pictures and carvings of animals to make magic—magic that would help them when they went hunting. These people may have thought that if they stabbed an animal's picture with a spearpoint, they would be able to kill the real animal more easily. So, perhaps the scars on some paintings were made by spearpoints. Perhaps the painted marks stand for spears or arrows flying at the animals. Perhaps the red spots stand for drops of blood.

However, other scientists point out that the pictures may not have been for magic at all. Maybe

the dots stand for falling rain, not blood. Maybe the pointed marks are supposed to show blowing wind. Maybe the scars were made simply to spoil the pictures for some reason.

Another odd thing about the cave paintings and carvings is that many of them were done on top of one another. A painting of a horse may have a painting of a mammoth partly covering it. A carving of a deer may have another deer carved right over it. Yet there's often plenty of space on the cave wall nearby for artists to have made separate paintings or carvings if they wished to. Why did they paint or carve over other paintings or carvings this way? Was there perhaps some magical reason?

Still another strange thing is that nearly all the paintings and carvings show only animals. There are very few paintings of people and none at all of plants. Did prehistoric people simply like animals—or did the animals stand for something else? Were they supposed to be spirits, or gods, or something we can't even guess at now?

Yes, there are many mysteries about the prehistoric paintings and sculptures in caves. Today, we can only guess at the reasons for all these things. There is no way we can figure out what went on in the minds of the artists who painted and carved on the walls of caves thousands of years ago.

Dinosaur Mysteries

What Killed All the Dinosaurs?

In a patch of forest by the side of a broad river, a number of gigantic animals are feeding on tree leaves. These animals are nearly three times taller than a human! Their big bodies are covered with scales, and their long jaws are shaped like the bill of a duck. As they munch, they constantly turn their heads, looking anxiously in every direction for dangerous enemies that prowl the forest. One kind of enemy is a huge, scaly creature whose enormous jaws are full of sharp, curved teeth six inches (15 centimeters) long.

Out beyond the forest spreads a vast plain where herds of other huge creatures graze. These are bulky, four-footed animals. Each has a pair of sharp horns jutting from its forehead, and a single short, sharp horn on its nose. The plain is also a

hunting ground for packs of small, two-legged, sharp-toothed flesh-eaters that dash about rapidly in search of prey.

This was the world of 70 million years ago—the world of those strange creatures we call dinosaurs. The dinosaurs were scaly skinned reptiles, related to the reptiles of today—lizards, snakes, turtles, alligators, and crocodiles. There were more than eight hundred different kinds of dinosaurs. Some were gigantic beasts as much as a hundred feet (30 meters) long. Others were no bigger than a chicken. From about 200 million to 65 million years ago—a total of 135 million years—these creatures ruled the land.

But by 64 million years ago there was not a dinosaur left! Something killed every one of these animals, as well as many other kinds of animals that lived in the world then. One of the biggest questions scientists have today is—what happened? What killed all the dinosaurs?

There are lots of ideas about this, of course. Some people think the dinosaurs died out because they were just too big, slow, clumsy, and stupid to survive. But this idea doesn't make any sense. For one thing, not all dinosaurs were big and slow. Many of them were small and quick. And most of them were no more stupid than the reptiles of today, while some were apparently a lot smarter. Actually, the dinosaurs were very successful creatures that survived for more than 130 million years. They were able to survive in their world just as well as other kinds of animals survive in today's world.

Another idea is that a sudden change in Earth's climate, from warm to cold, killed all the dinosaurs. The dinosaurs were reptiles, and cold weather makes reptiles lazyish and barely able to move. A long period of cold weather will kill them.

However, if the climate had grown cold enough to kill the dinosaurs, it would have been cold enough to kill all the other kinds of reptiles, too, including lizards, snakes, turtles, alligators, and crocodiles. All these kinds of reptiles lived at the same time as the dinosaurs and are still living in the world today. So it doesn't seem likely that there was a "cold spell." In fact, all the evidence shows that the world stayed quite warm long after the dinosaurs were all gone. Thus it wasn't cold weather that killed them.

Some scientists think that the world may have suddenly gotten too hot, and this killed the dinosaurs. Scientists can tell that there were some tremendous volcanic eruptions about 65 million years ago, and this would have filled the air with a kind of gas called carbon dioxide. A lot of this gas in the air would have prevented heat from escaping from Earth into space, as it usually does. The trapped heat would have caused the air to get much hotter. Just as reptiles cannot take cold, neither can they take too much heat—it kills them. So, if the world did heat up for a while, that could, indeed, have killed the dinosaurs.

However, the same thing that's wrong with the "too cold" idea is also wrong with the "too hot" one. If the world had become hot enough to kill all the dinosaurs, all the other reptiles would have been killed, too—but a lot of them are still around. Most scientists don't think the climate ever got hot enough to cause reptiles any trouble.

Still another idea is that some form of disease killed the dinosaurs. The trouble with this idea is that a disease simply doesn't attack all different kinds of creatures. A disease such as smallpox, which once killed many people, never bothered dogs, cats, or horses. Many kinds of dinosaurs were as different from one another as dogs or cats or horses are from people. So, while a disease might have killed one or more kinds of dinosaurs, it couldn't have killed all kinds.

Some scientists believe that an exploding star far out in space might have killed the dinosaurs. The kind of exploding star called a supernova gives off much the same sort of radiation as an atomic bomb—radiation that can kill living things. If Earth were in the path of such radiation, the dinosaurs could have been killed.

The trouble with the idea is that radiation from a supernova would have killed almost everything. Scientists wonder how so many kinds of creatures could have survived if such a thing had happened. They think it wouldn't have been possible for radiation to affect only dinosaurs and a few other kinds of creatures and spare everything else.

One of the newest ideas is that the dinosaurs died out as a result of a comet or a huge meteorite that came hurtling out of space and smashed into Earth. There is evidence that this may have happened about 65 million years ago.

Scientists say that if it did happen, a huge meteorite smashing into the ground would have thrown tons and tons of dust into the air. This would have made the sky nearly as dark as night for several months. Of course, with no sunlight in the sky for so long a time, most of the plants on Earth would have died. With no plants to eat, all the plant-eating dinosaurs would have died. And with no plant-eaters to feed on, the meat-eaters would soon have died out, too.

However, even if such an event did occur, many scientists wonder why, if conditions were bad enough to kill all the dinosaurs, so many other kinds of creatures survived.

So, there are certain objections to all of these ideas. Even though scientists have tried for over a hundred years to figure out what killed all the dinosaurs, no one has yet thought of a reason that seems to be right.

Were Dinosaurs Warm-Blooded?

Could you have outrun a hungry *Tyrannosaurus* (tih ran uh SAWR uhs)—or would it have quickly caught you and gobbled you up?

Tyrannosaurus and the other dinosaurs were reptiles. Anyone who has ever watched one of today's reptiles knows that most of these creatures are usually very slow moving and lazyish. A turtle or an alligator will often lie in the same place for hours without making the slightest move, even

though it is wide awake. And when a turtle, alligator, or other reptile walks, it generally plods along, taking all the time in the world.

Reptiles tend to be slow moving and lazyish because they are cold-blooded, have a small, rather smooth brain, and have sprawling legs. On the other hand, the quick-moving animals called mammals (such as dogs, cats, and humans) are warm-blooded. They tend to have a large, more wrinkled brain (which helps make them smarter) and straight legs.

A warm-blooded creature's body is heated from inside and is almost always the same temperature. This steady warmth helps the creature stay lively and quick. But the body of a cold-blooded animal is heated from the outside, by the air or water around it. The lower the temperature of the air or water, the lower the temperature of the cold-blooded animal. A low body temperature makes the creature stiff and slow. After a cool night, a snake or lizard is generally so stiff it can barely stir. It has to lie in hot sunlight until its body warms up enough so that it can move easily again.

Were the dinosaurs slow moving, like the reptiles of today? For a long time, most scientists thought so. They felt that huge, bulky, plant-eating dinosaurs such as *Brachiosaurus* (brak ee uh SAWR uhs) and *Apatosaurus* (ap uh tuh SAWR uhs), also called *Brontosaurus* (brahn tuh SAWR uhs), probably had to spend most of their time in the warm water of a swamp or river to keep themselves warm and active. Big flesh-eating dinosaurs such as *Tyrannosaurus* and *Allosaurus* (al uh SAWR uhs) probably prowled about slowly or lay in wait for a chance to make a short, clumsy rush at a plant-eating dinosaur that had ambled up onto land.

Then, scientists began to make discoveries that changed their minds. They found that many dinosaurs were apparently rather quick moving. And some scientists began to wonder if perhaps dinosaurs were actually warm-blooded instead of cold-blooded like today's reptiles. The reptiles we know today seem very different from the dinosaurs.

For one thing, a reptile of today, such as a lizard or turtle, stands with its legs sprawled out to its sides and its body resting on the ground. To move, it actually creeps, usually dragging its body and tail. But by measuring the legs of dinosaur skeletons and the distance between dinosaur footprints, and by examining the bones in the tails of dinosaurs, scientists have found that many dinosaurs stood and walked with their legs straight beneath them and their tails off the ground. This is the way a cat, dog, or other warm-blooded creature walks.

Furthermore, most dinosaurs had legs that were quite long in proportion to the rest of their bodies. Long legs mean that an animal can run fast for a long time. But, as far as is known, only warm-blooded animals can do that.

Another reason that some scientists think dinosaurs may have been warm-blooded is because of the way their bones are formed. The bones of most warm-blooded mammals have many small blood vessels running through them. Dinosaur bones do, too. But the bones of most cold-blooded reptiles do not have these blood vessels.

There seem to be good reasons for thinking that dinosaurs might have been warm-blooded. And many scientists believe they were. However, just as many scientists think dinosaurs were cold-blooded, and there are good reasons for that, too.

Experiments with alligators have shown that large reptiles tend to heat up or cool off slowly. Many dinosaurs were gigantic, of course. Because they lived in a warm climate, the temperature of their bodies would never have changed very much. Thus, they could have stayed warm enough to be fairly fast moving without being warm-blooded.

For another thing, the teeth of today's cold-blooded reptiles form rings, just like the rings in a tree trunk. The teeth of warm-blooded animals do not form such rings. Scientists have found that dinosaur teeth have rings, which seems to show that dinosaurs must have been cold-blooded.

Still another bit of evidence is that a number of kinds of dinosaurs had fins or "plates" on their bodies. Such things usually help an animal soak up heat from sunlight or let heat out in order to cool off. Cold-blooded animals need such things, but warm-blooded animals do not. It seems likely that dinosaurs with fins and plates needed to lie quietly in sun or shade to warm up or cool off, just as most reptiles do today.

And, finally, fossil "molds" of some dinosaur brains have been found. For the most part, they showed that dinosaur brains were small and rather smooth, much like the brains of today's cold-blooded reptiles.

So, while there seems to be good evidence that dinosaurs might have been warm-blooded, quick, and clever, there is just as much evidence that they may have been cold-blooded, rather slow, and stupid. No one knows for sure which they were. There's no way to tell whether a *Tyrannosaurus* just plodded along—slowly enough for you to get away if one were chasing you—or whether it could quickly catch you and have you for lunch!

Fortunately, you'll never have to worry about it!

Are Birds Really Dinosaurs?

You'll probably be surprised to learn that at this very minute a dinosaur may be running about on your lawn! This could be true if a robin or sparrow or other bird is on your lawn right now. For some scientists believe that birds are a kind of dinosaur!

The reason for this belief is a creature called *Archaeopteryx* (ahr kee AHP tuhr ihks), which means "ancient wing." It lived about 140 million years ago, during the time of the dinosaurs. One of these creatures chanced to drown in a sea, and its body sank into the soft mud at the sea bottom. Over many millions of years the mud hardened into rock. The rock had a perfect imprint of the *Archaeopteryx*'s bones and body pressed into it, like a footprint preserved in a concrete sidewalk. About 125 years ago, scientists found this imprint. They have been studying it ever since.

From its bones, *Archaeopteryx* looked just like a small dinosaur. It had long jaws filled with sharp teeth; a long, lizardlike tail; and tiny, clawed "hands." If this creature's bones had been all that was found, scientists would have agreed that it was a little dinosaur, about the size of a crow.

But there was more to the imprint in the stone than that. The imprint showed that *Archaeopteryx*'s body had been covered with feathers. It had long feathers on its tail and long feathers on its arms, forming wings. Because of the feathers, scientists decided that even though *Archaeopteryx* had teeth and clawed hands, it must have been a bird—probably the first kind of bird.

Archaeopteryx was a bird, but it was so much like a reptile that scientists are positive its ancestors were reptiles. The question is, what kind of reptile? Some scientists think its ancestors were little reptiles called thecodonts (THEE kuh dahnts).

But other scientists feel that *Archaeopteryx* was so much like a dinosaur that its ancestors—and the ancestors of all birds—must have been dinosaurs. And many of these scientists say that if the ancestors of birds were dinosaurs, then birds are actually just a kind of dinosaur. Some even think they should be called dinosaurs instead of birds. If this happens, perhaps people will put up dinosaur houses instead of birdhouses!

Of course, scientists don't all agree on this, and perhaps they never will. But someday, someone may prove that birds are descended from dinosaurs and are, indeed, a kind of dinosaur.

What Color Were Dinosaurs?

No human being ever saw a live dinosaur. Dinosaurs died out millions of years before humans appeared. Yet, books are filled with pictures of dinosaurs, and there are life-sized models of dinosaurs in museums. How do we know what these creatures looked like?

We can tell how a dinosaur was shaped by the shape of its skeleton. We know what dinosaur skin was like because there are fossils of dinosaur skin—chunks of rock with imprints of dinosaur skin that was pressed into the rock when it was soft clay. But the real problem is color. There's no way to tell what color an animal was from bare bones or from a skin print.

However, scientists have a way of working out what colors different kinds of dinosaurs might have been. They know that dinosaurs were reptiles, so they base the colors of dinosaurs on the colors of reptiles that are living today.

Crocodiles are among the largest living reptiles. And dinosaurs were descended from reptiles that

We can make models of dinosaurs that show their exact size, shape, and skin appearance. But we have no way of knowing what color a dinosaur was.

Dinosaur skin that has turned to stone, such as this Anatosaurus fossil, shows us what the skin of a live dinosaur looked like, but not the coloring.

were a lot like crocodiles. So, it's a pretty safe guess that many of the larger dinosaurs were probably colored much like crocodiles—backs and sides blotched with brown, yellow, and black, and undersides that were yellow or pale tan. However, the larger the dinosaurs, the duller the colors probably became. The biggest dinosaurs, such as *Apatosaurus* (ap uh tuh SAWR uhs), also called *Brontosaurus* (brahn tuh SAWR uhs), probably looked almost solid brown or gray, just as our biggest animals, whales and elephants, are solid colors.

Small dinosaurs that ate plants and lived in forests were probably colored much like forest-dwelling lizards of today. They would have been camouflaged with blotches of green, black, yellow, and brown. In a dim green forest with broken-up patches of sunlight and shadow, these colors would make them hard to see.

Some small flesh-eating dinosaurs hunted their prey by running swiftly after it. They probably lived in much the same way as the leopard, cheetah, and other hunting cats of today. So, most scientists think these dinosaurs were probably colored much as those cats are, with tan or orange bodies and patterns of black, dark brown, or white.

Although scientists keep coming up with new ways of finding things out, we'll probably never know for sure what color dinosaurs were. But most scientists think the colors they have figured out for dinosaurs are probably pretty close.

Historical Mysteries

Who Really Discovered America?

The captain of the ship stepped out of his cabin and stopped short. A large group of sailors stood before him. From their angry and stubborn looks, the captain knew he could be in for trouble. He had promised these men fame and wealth when they reached the land that was the ship's destination. For some days now, he had told them they would soon sight land. But the ship had been at sea for thirty-five days, and there was no sign of land. The captain knew the men no longer believed him. They were worried and angry, and might mutiny!

"Do you have something you want to say to me?" he asked.

"Aye, Captain, that we do," answered one of the sailors. "We've come twice as far on this sea as any sailor ever did before. You were sure we'd sight land by now, but we haven't. We think we've done enough. We want to turn back for home while we still have enough food and water to get there!"

The captain said nothing for a moment, but he

was thinking rapidly. He felt sure they would sight land at any time. He could not bear the thought of turning back when he knew success was so near. He would rather die! He had to convince the crew to give him just a little more time.

The captain was Christopher Columbus. He did manage to talk the men into giving him more time—three more days—and everyone knows what happened. Early on the morning of October 12, 1492, they sighted land.

Columbus thought he had arrived at islands off the coast of Japan, which is what he had set out to do. But the islands were actually off a huge, and at that time unknown, land mass lying between Europe and Asia. This land mass was, of course, what we now call North and South America. For hundreds of years, Christopher Columbus was given credit as the man who discovered this "New World."

But today we know that Columbus was not the first explorer to reach America. And even during Columbus' own time many people thought someone else was the true discoverer of America.

Columbus did not actually reach the continent of what is now South America until August 1498. Until then, he had really discovered only some islands. But an Italian-born explorer named Amerigo Vespucci (am ehr EE goh veh SPOO chee) claimed to have reached the southern continent in

1497, and many people believed him. Thus, when mapmakers began producing maps of the New World, they called it *America* in honor of Amerigo Vespucci.

Historians do not believe that Vespucci really did get to South America before Columbus. But we know that at least one other European reached America long before Columbus and Vespucci were born. And there may have been others who came even earlier!

In about the year 1002, a Norse seaman named Leif Ericson, sailing from Greenland, reached the coast of North America. At one of the places where he and his men landed, they found many grapevines. They made wine from the grapes, and called the place Vinland, or "wineland." They spent a winter in Vinland, building a big house for themselves and a shed to protect their ship.

No one now knows exactly where Vinland was, but in 1961 scientists found the remains of a Norse settlement on the coast of Newfoundland, Canada. Most scientists and historians think this was probably close to where Leif and his men landed. At any rate, those Norse sailors reached part of America almost five hundred years before Columbus.

However, there are some people who believe that Leif Ericson wasn't the first European to reach America. There is an old tale, *Voyage of Brendan*, which tells how an Irish priest named Brendan and some monks sailed into the Atlantic Ocean around

the year 550. They found an island which became known as St. Brendan's Island.

No one knows for sure where this island was, but some people believe that it may have been North America. They say that Brendan and the others simply didn't realize that it was a continent, not an island. Thus, it is possible that the first Europeans to reach America were Irishmen who got there almost five hundred years before Leif Ericson and his Norsemen. Most scientists and historians think this is very unlikely.

But even if Brendan did get to America more than fourteen hundred years ago, some people believe he wasn't the first anyway. They think he was beaten by explorers from China! There is some evidence for this.

Official Chinese written records of the year 499 tell how a crew of seamen and a Buddhist monk named Hoei-sin sailed east from China and found a new land. They called it Fusang, because it had

This huge stone head, found in Mexico, was carved about three thousand years ago. Some people think it may be a sculpture of an African sailor who discovered America.

many trees that resembled a Chinese tree known as the fusang. An old Chinese map shows Fusang lying east of China, far beyond Japan—just about where America would be. Some people think Fusang may be present-day Mexico.

A number of people, some of them scientists, believe that explorers from North Africa first visited America about 2,500 years ago! Some carved stones, found in Canada, seem to show that sailors from the ancient city of Carthage reached Canada about 500 B.C. The writing carved on the stones is in the language of the Carthaginians. But most scientists think the stones are fakes.

Some people think that other sailors from Africa may have reached Central America as much as three thousand years ago—about 1,000 B.C.! The reason for this belief is a number of huge stone heads, nearly three thousand years old, that have been dug up on the coast of Mexico. These heads, which are about eight feet (2.4 meters) high, look very much like the heads of African men. Some people say the heads are sculptures of ancient African sailors who reached what is now Mexico and became kings or chiefs among the Indians.

There are many claims—Spanish, Norse, Irish, Chinese, Carthaginian, and African—for the discovery of America. But, actually, there is no question as to who first discovered America. The ancestors of the American Indians came to North America from Asia about thirty thousand years ago. So, they were first—by thousands of years.

What Became of the Neanderthal People?

Imagine that you are standing on a high hill in northern Europe. You are looking at the countryside spread out before you—but the time is fifty thousand years ago, and the Ice Age holds the world in its grip.

The sky is gray and filled with whirling snowflakes. Deep snow covers the land as far as you can see. In the distance spreads the dark green mass of a forest of fir trees. Near its edge you can see a dozen reddish-brown shapes. They are a herd of mastodons—big elephants covered with shaggy fur. And far, far away, a gleaming, grayish-white band stretches across the horizon. It is the edge of a gigantic sheet of ice that spreads for thousands of miles across the northern part of the land.

This was the world of the prehistoric people that are known as Neanderthals. They are named after the Neander Valley in West Germany, where some of their bones were first discovered. For many thousands of years, generations of these people were born, grew up, lived, and died in this cold, snowy world. They hunted mastodons, woolly rhinoceroses, and many other beasts. They kept themselves warm and comfortable in caves and shelters. They successfully survived the Ice Age.

The Neanderthals were not quite like us. They had shorter, stockier bodies with heavy bones. They were probably a lot stronger than most people are now. Their chins did not stick out as ours do, but sloped back. Their brow ridges—where the eyebrows are—stuck out over their eyes, their heads were longer than ours, and they had bigger teeth and slightly bigger brains than we do. However, if you could see Neanderthal people dressed in modern clothes, you probably wouldn't notice such differences. These people really didn't look very different from many people of today.

The Neanderthals were smart and skillful. From a kind of hard stone called flint, they made several kinds of tools. They had sharp-edged knives for cutting meat, skins, and wood, as well as sharp points for making holes in things. They also made scrapers for smoothing wood and scraping hides clean. They knew how to make fire. They made clothing out of animal hides. And they built hutlike shelters out of tree branches and animal skins.

Although the Neanderthals lived long ago, in a harsh, brutal world, they don't seem to have been just rough, wild savages. We know that they took care of crippled people, and very old people who couldn't hunt or help themselves. They buried their dead in graves, with special ceremonies. They may have had some kind of religion. Although they didn't make paintings or carvings, they apparently had a sense of beauty. Some of them collected pretty things, such as shiny stones and snail shells.

Yes, the Neanderthal people were smart, skillful, sensitive survivors. They made their way successfully in a harsh, cold, snowy world for some forty-five thousand years. But then something happened—and it's one of the great mysteries for scientists who study the ancient world. It seems that the Neanderthals disappeared about thirty-five thousand years ago. In their place appeared a very different kind of people—people who were very much like the people of today.

What happened to the Neanderthals? And where did these new people, called Cro-Magnons (kro MAG nahns), come from? (The Cro-Magnons are named for a cave in France where their skeletons were first found.)

Scientists have worked out several possible answers to the mystery of the vanishing Neanderthals and the more or less sudden appearance of the Cro-Magnons. One is that when

Neanderthal man

Cro-Magnon man

there was a temporary warming period about thirty-five thousand years ago, the Neanderthal people began to change, or *adapt*, as scientists say, in order to survive in a different, warmer world. Some scientists believe they just slowly changed into people like us. Thus, they disappeared because they became something else.

Another idea is that the Cro-Magnon people slowly spread out across Europe, Asia, and Africa. If so, two things might have happened.

One is that Neanderthals and Cro-Magnons might have mixed together, with both kinds of men and women marrying one another. After a while, the descendants of Neanderthals and Cro-Magnons would have looked much alike. Thus, once again, the Neanderthals would have disappeared because they changed.

A second possibility is that Neanderthals and Cro-Magnons were rivals, and the Neanderthals could not hold their own against the Cro-Magnons. The Cro-Magnons made better tools and weapons and had more advanced ways. So, they might have taken over more and more places and crowded the Neanderthals out. The Neanderthals might have slowly disappeared.

As time goes on, scientists may learn which of these possibilities is right. But at this moment, no one knows for sure what happened to the Neanderthal people.

Was There a Real King Arthur?

The story of King Arthur of Britain and his knights of the Round Table is one of the greatest stories in the English language. It is the kind of story called an epic—a grand, majestic, powerful tale of great heroism and adventure.

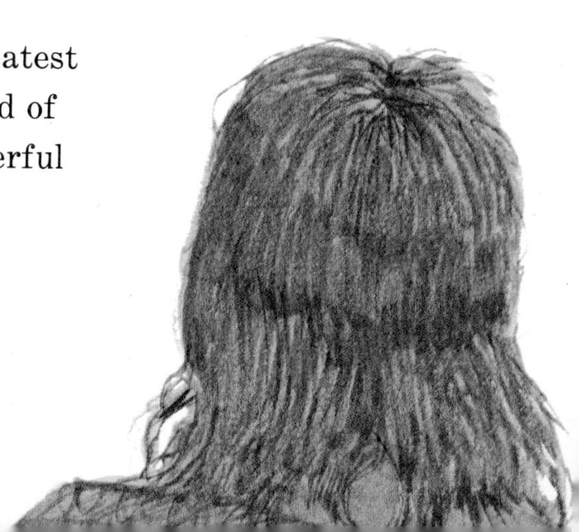

According to the legend, Arthur, who lived long ago in the days of knights and castles, was an orphan who was brought up by a British knight. When Arthur was a young man, the king of Britain died without a son or relative to take his place. The people could not decide who should rule them. Britain faced grim civil war as different noblemen prepared to fight to make themselves king.

Then, there magically appeared a huge stone with a sword stuck in it. A message carved on the stone said that whoever could pull out the sword was the rightful king. Many noblemen tried to remove the sword, but none could do so. Arthur happened to see the sword. Without even knowing about the carved message, he easily pulled the sword out of the stone. Everyone accepted him as the new king.

King Arthur believed it was his duty to see that all his people had justice and happiness. He gathered together a group of strong, brave knights—such men as Sir Lancelot, Sir Gawain, Sir Percival, and Sir Galahad—to help him keep Britain free of evil and injustice, and to protect the people. With the help of these knights of the Round Table and of Merlin, a powerful wizard, Arthur kept out the Saxons who were trying to invade Britain. He also got rid of many evil nobles, wizards, and sorceresses who mistreated people and caused trouble.

Arthur managed to keep his people safe and happy for many years. But then he was betrayed by his own son, Modred. Because of Modred's plottings, the knights of the Round Table broke up into two groups, one led by Modred and one by Arthur.

In a terrible battle between the two groups, Modred was killed and Arthur was so badly wounded it seemed certain he would die. He was taken away to an unknown place by three sorceresses and never seen again. So the days of peace, happiness, and justice in Britain came to an end. But, according to the legend, someday when

Britain faces its greatest peril, King Arthur will return to save it.

The legend of King Arthur is a marvelous story, but it's also something of a mystery. Many historians and scientists think that the figure of King Arthur is based on a real person. Some of them have been working for years to find out who that person was.

The King Arthur legend goes back in history to a time we don't know much about—England some fifteen hundred years ago. At that time, England, or Britannia as it was then called, was part of the

Roman Empire and was protected by a Roman army. But Rome began to have serious troubles, and the army in Britain was called home. Britain soon split up into many little kingdoms that began to quarrel and war with one another. Then Britain was invaded by warriors from Scotland.

To keep these invaders from taking over his land, the king of one of the little British kingdoms hired an army of warriors from Germany. This army, formed of warriors from three German tribes—Angles, Saxons, and Jutes—beat back the invasion from Scotland. But then the German warriors stayed in Britain, sent for their wives and children, and began conquering the country for themselves!

From what we know, it must have been a dreadful time for the people of Britain. A peaceful farmer never knew when his home might be attacked by a Saxon war party and he and all his family killed. The people in cities lived in fear that they might be besieged—surrounded and attacked by an army of the invaders. That could mean slow starvation and then the destruction of the city and the death of most of its people.

But apparently, just when things looked worst, an army of British warriors under a bold, skillful leader began to battle the invaders. The Angles, Saxons, and Jutes began to suffer defeat and be pushed out of places they had conquered. And the man who led this victorious British army may have been the man later known as King Arthur.

There is some evidence for this. About twelve hundred years ago, a British historian known as Nennius wrote a book called *History of the Britons.* In this book, Nennius said that about three hundred years earlier there was a British general named Arthur who fought for British kings against the German invaders.

Many stories and folk tales told by people in parts of Britain about a thousand years ago are about a great king called Arthur. About 850 years ago, a man known as Geoffrey of Monmouth put some of those stories into a book called *The History of the Kings of Britain.* Geoffrey wrote that Arthur was a British king who not only defeated the invading Scots and Germans, but who also conquered Ireland, Iceland, and most of Europe. Geoffrey was the first to tell about the treachery of Modred and the terrible battle in which Modred was killed and Arthur mortally wounded.

As time went on, many other writers and poets added to the legend of Arthur. They put in the parts about wizards, sorceresses, the Round Table, and the quest for the Holy Grail. Historians know that none of these stories are true, but they think that other parts of the Arthurian legend may be true.

For example, according to the stories, King Arthur had a great castle at a place called Camelot. No one today knows exactly where Camelot might have been, but many people have thought it was probably a place in England now known as Cadbury Hill. And in the 1960's, scientists dug up the remains of what seems to be a large, imposing fortress there. They found that it belonged to the time of Arthur, just about fifteen hundred years ago. Could this old fortress actually have been Arthur's Camelot?

In recent years, an even more exciting discovery was made. Historians have long known of a British leader called Riothamus, who lived at about the time Arthur was supposed to have lived and who did many of the things Geoffrey of Monmouth said

Arthur had done. It didn't seem possible that Riothamus could have been Arthur, because their names are so different. But now scholars have found that Riothamus is not a name. It is a *title* that means "high king." So perhaps this man was the real Arthur!

Of course, some historians and scientists don't think there was a real King Arthur. They think Arthur is just a made-up hero that people began telling stories about long ago. But many others think that King Arthur was a real person—a brave and clever general or king who saved his land from invasion, brought his people peace and justice, and was so admired that he has been remembered for fifteen centuries. And they think that someday they may find out who this man was.

What Became of the "Lost Colony"?

Some four hundred years ago, on a May day in 1587, three small, wooden ships set sail from England and headed out into the Atlantic Ocean. More than two months later they arrived at tiny Roanoke Island off the northeastern coast of what is now North Carolina.

On the ships, groups of men, women, and children stared eagerly, and perhaps a bit fearfully, at the island's shoreline. They had come from a land of houses, farms, roads, villages, and crowded cities, but here they saw only vast, thick, wild forest. They knew that wild animals roamed the woods. And on the mainland, separated from the island by only a few miles (kilometers) of water, there were hordes of people known as Indians. This land was not a bit like safe, settled, law-abiding old England! It was a wild, untamed, and very dangerous land!

However, it was now to be home for these people. They intended to settle on Roanoke Island and become the first permanent colony of English people in North America. Another group of English people had tried to start a colony on the island a few years earlier, but most had given up and returned to England. The people of this second group—91 men, 17 women, and 9 children—were determined not to fail.

They took over the log houses the first colonists had built. The houses had been sitting open and empty for a year, so the people scrubbed and swept and dusted, cleaning out dead leaves and sending spiders and other tiny creatures scurrying. Everyone must have been greatly excited on this first day in a new land. The children probably darted and dashed about with wide eyes, calling to one another as they made new discoveries.

A little less than a month later, a baby girl was born to two of the colonists, Ellinor White Dare and Ananias Dare. The part of America to which Roanoke Island then belonged was called Virginia.

So, the baby girl was named after the land—Virginia Dare. She was the first English child born in North America.

About the time Virginia Dare was born, the colony began to run into trouble. The food brought on the ships wouldn't be enough to last the winter. The colonists wouldn't be able to begin growing their own food until next spring. Unless they got more food, they might all starve.

It was decided that the colony's leader, John White, should return to England when the three ships sailed back, and buy food for the colony. White and the others agreed that if the people ran out of food or had some other trouble while he was gone, they would go to get help from one of the

nearby Indian tribes. If this happened, they would leave a message for White—they would carve the name of the place where they had gone on a house door or on a tree.

On August 27, John White left for England. It was fall by the time he got there, and he spent the rest of the year gathering supplies. He intended to return to Roanoke in the early spring.

But when the spring of 1588 arrived, White found that he could not leave England. War had broken out between England and Spain. A gigantic Spanish fleet had sailed to invade England! The English defeated the Spanish, but John White was not able to return to Roanoke until August of 1590, three years after he had left. With some of the men from the ship that had brought him, he hurried to the little settlement.

It was gone! The houses had all been taken down. There was no sign of anyone. But carved on one tree were the letters CRO, and on another the word CROATOAN.

John White was not particularly worried. He knew that Croatoan was the name of a nearby island where a small tribe of friendly Indians lived. He and the others decided to sail there the next day to look for the colonists.

But that night a storm broke. The ship's anchor cable snapped, and the ship began to drift. Some of its supplies of food and water were damaged.

The men decided they didn't dare try to set out to look for the colonists in a damaged ship, without enough food and water. Sadly, they headed for the nearby West Indies, and from there for England. John White was never able to return to America, and no one else went to look for the colonists. Not one of the people, including little Virginia Dare, was ever seen or heard of again. The colony on Roanoke Island became known as the "Lost Colony."

The story of the Lost Colony became a mysterious part of American history. For hundreds of years many Americans wondered what happened to those 117 people. Did the Indians kill them, as some of the Virginia Indians said? Did Spanish soldiers discover the colony and carry all the colonists off as captives? Or, as a few people have fancied, did something weird and terrible happen to them?

Today, many historians think there is a very simple answer. They think the colonists ran out of food and joined the friendly Indians on Croatoan (or Croatan) Island, just as they had planned. When no one came to find them, the colonists simply became part of the Indian tribe—and their descendants are living in North Carolina this very day!

There are good reasons for believing this. For one thing, when people from England came to that part of North Carolina again many years later, they were astounded to find a group of English-speaking people already there. But these English-speaking people didn't call themselves Englishmen. They called themselves Croatan—which was the name of the island to which John White thought the colonists had gone.

These Croatan people seemed to be Indians. But, unlike other Indians, many of them had blond hair and blue eyes, as many English people do. Many of

These scientists are searching for traces of the Lost Colony. They especially hope to find clues that will show where the people of the colony went.

them also had English names, such as Jones, Brooks, and Sampson—and these were the same as the names of the Roanoke colonists!

The descendants of the Croatan people are known as Lumbee Indians. They now live in southeastern North Carolina, near the city of Lumberton. There are about forty thousand Lumbee people, many of whom believe they are the descendants of the English settlers. A number of historians agree with them. So, perhaps the mystery of the Lost Colony is solved. Perhaps the colony was never lost at all, but simply went off and joined the Indians!

Did Explorers from Space Ever Visit Earth?

Some people believe that explorers from outer space visited Earth long ago. Is there evidence of such a visit? If so, what is it?

Some of the supposed evidence comes from the ancient kingdom of Babylonia, in the Near East. Stories and pictures, thousands of years old, tell of a strange creature called Oannes, who was half human and half fish. According to the stories, Oannes came out of the sea each day to talk to the Babylonian wise men. He supposedly taught the Babylonians how to write, how to plant crops, and how to build houses. He also taught them mathematics and astronomy. Each night he returned to the sea.

Some people now think that Oannes was a "spaceman"—a creature from some watery planet far away. They think he had his spacecraft "parked" in the sea, because he was a fishlike creature and needed to be in water part of the time. And they say that because he came from a civilization advanced enough to build spacecraft, he knew a great deal more than the ancient Babylonians and could teach them many things.

But this really isn't very good evidence. The story of Oannes sounds very much like a fairy tale.

And there isn't anything in it that says Oannes came from space. Ancient people such as the Babylonians believed in many gods and monsters. It looks very much as if Oannes were a made-up monster. There is certainly no proof that any such creature ever lived.

Other supposed evidence comes from Central America, where the Mayan people lived about 1,700 years ago. The Mayans had a great civilization. They had a kind of picture writing, and they knew a lot about mathematics and astronomy. Some people believe that visitors from space taught all these things to the Mayans. Their main evidence for this belief is an ancient Mayan picture—a picture carved in stone. It seems to show a man in a tight-fitting space suit, with a kind of helmet on his head, at the controls of a spaceship. Some people believe this is a picture of one of the space explorers who taught the Mayans.

However, scientists who have spent many years studying the ways of the Mayans say that the picture is no such thing. The man isn't wearing a space suit at all. He is bare-chested and barelegged, as most Mayan men were. The "helmet" isn't a helmet—it's the way Mayan men wore their hair. And the man is not at the controls of a spaceship, but at an altar—the same kind of altar shown on many Mayan carvings. It seems, then, that the stone carving isn't evidence of any visitors from space.

Some people think this ancient Mayan carving shows an astronaut in a spacecraft. Scientists say that it actually shows a Mayan man beneath an altar shaped like a tree.

Still more supposed evidence comes from the Republic of Mali, in Africa, where a tribe of people called the Dogon live. About forty years ago, some visiting scientists were amazed to discover that the priests of the Dogon religion knew more about astronomy than seemed possible, for the Dogon people had never had any telescopes.

The priests knew that the planet Jupiter has moons, and that the planet Saturn has rings around it. They also knew that the star called Sirius, which is the brightest star in the sky, is orbited by a small, heavy object that takes fifty years to go around it. The Dogon priests couldn't possibly have found out about these things without a powerful telescope. But the priests insisted that the Dogon people have known these things for more than eight hundred years—which is about 450 years before the invention of the telescope.

For some people, this is proof that creatures from space visited the Dogon tribe long ago and told them these things. These people say that there doesn't seem to be any other way the Dogons could have gotten such information. Astronomers have known about Jupiter's moons and Saturn's rings for only some three hundred years, and about Sirius' companion for a little more than a hundred years.

However, some of the things the Dogon priests tell about aren't correct. According to their knowledge, Jupiter has four moons—but actually it has sixteen. It seems as if "space explorers" would have known the true number of moons. The priests also believe that Sirius has two companions. If so, astronomers have yet to discover this second companion.

So, most scientists don't feel that the Dogon priests' knowledge of astronomy proves they were visited by space explorers at all. It is possible that Dogon priests learned about Jupiter's moons and Saturn's rings from some European explorer two or three hundred years ago—not eight hundred years ago, as the present-day Dogon priests believe. And during the past hundred years, priests could have heard about Sirius' companion.

Almost all scientists agree that explorers from space *could* have visited Earth hundreds or thousands of years ago. But they don't think there is any evidence that this happened.

Was There a Real Atlantis?

More than two thousand years ago, in ancient Greece, there lived a man named Aristocles. He was generally known by the nickname Plato, which means "broad shouldered." Plato was a teacher and writer. People today look upon him as one of the greatest thinkers in all history.

One of the books Plato wrote was a kind of history of his part of the world from very ancient times. In this work, Plato told of a great power, the empire of Atlantis. According to Plato, Atlantis

was a huge island that lay in the Atlantic Ocean. Its armies conquered and enslaved most of Europe. Finally the army of the Greek city of Athens defeated Atlantis in a terrible battle. Then, according to Plato,

> "... There occurred violent earthquakes and floods; and in a single day and night of misfortune ... the island of Atlantis disappeared in the depths of the sea."

All this is supposed to have happened some nine thousand years before Plato's time. The disaster he wrote about seems very real. For centuries, people who read Plato's story wondered if it were true. They also wondered just where Atlantis had been.

During the past hundred years or so, many people have become interested in Atlantis and tried to find out more about it. One man felt there was evidence that Atlantis had been part of the coast of Africa. Another believed Atlantis had been a large island in the North Sea. Still another claimed to have seen what seemed to be huge stone statues beneath the water in the Mediterranean Sea near Italy. He felt sure that these were ruins of Atlantis.

Several men wrote books describing the civilization of Atlantis and the way of life of its people. But these books were rather fanciful, for the writers claimed that Atlantis had a civilization that was as high as, or higher than, the civilization of our world today. The writers insisted that they could tell this from old legends and myths. Actually, they just made up most of what they wrote.

These huge stone blocks are on the sea bottom near Florida. When they were found, some people thought they were part of an ancient road, but they are actually a natural formation.

From time to time, things are discovered in the sea that look as if they might be ruins of Atlantis. But these always turn out to be something else. Divers once found what looked like a road under the water off the coast of Bimini, a tiny island in the Atlantic Ocean near Florida. Many large blocks of stone seemed to have been fitted together to make a long stretch of road. However, scientists examined the "road" carefully. They found it was just a stretch of what is known as "beach rock"—rock that naturally splits into square sections.

Most scientists don't think there ever was a big island in the Atlantic Ocean. They say there isn't any evidence of such a thing. They feel that Plato's story was just a legend.

However, a few scientists believe the story of Atlantis was based on something that really happened. In the Aegean Sea, between Greece and Turkey, there is a small island called Thira. There is evidence of a great disaster that took place there about 3,500 years ago, which would be more than a thousand years before Plato was born. A volcano on Thira blew up in a tremendous eruption. Much of the island sank into the sea.

In the 1960's, scientists dug up the ruins of a town and palace that had been buried beneath ash from the volcano. The titanic eruption destroyed what was evidently a rich and powerful civilization. This makes some scientists feel that Thira was the place Plato was writing about.

We may never know the truth about Atlantis.

Some people think it is just a legend. Others think the island of Thira was Atlantis. And a few people will probably always believe that at one time there really was a great island-continent in the Atlantic Ocean.

Solved Mysteries

The Terrifying Pongo

In 1613, a book called *Pilgrimages of the World* was published in England. It was filled with tales of trips to distant lands—lands unfamiliar to most English people at that time. One of the tales told of the adventures of a sailor named William Battel, one of the first Englishmen ever to go to Africa.

Battel described a terrifying monster he had seen in Africa—a creature the African people called a "Pongo." It was shaped like a human, wrote Battel, but it was much bigger. And it was stronger than ten men! It was covered with thick fur, except for its feet, hands, ears, and face. Battel wrote that Pongos lived in small groups and would kill people they met in the forest!

Some people who read Battel's tale of the Pongo wondered if this monster might be some kind of "wild man." Most people believed the tale, for people at that time generally believed almost anything.

However, two hundred years later, most scientists felt that Battel had made up his story of the giant, furry, humanlike monster. By this time, many parts of Africa had been explored by Europeans, and no one had ever seen any such thing as a Pongo. Nevertheless, some explorers told of hearing tales of huge, hairy, humanlike creatures that lived in the deepest parts of the forests. Despite what the scientists said, some people wondered if the mysterious Pongo might really exist.

Then, in 1846, an English missionary in Africa went to visit another missionary who showed him a strange, huge skull. African people told the two men it was the skull of a furry, humanlike creature that they feared more than a lion or any other fierce beast! The two missionaries later found several more skulls, which they bought and sent to a famous scientist in England to study.

Scientists who hadn't believed there was such a thing as a Pongo now realized there *was* a strange, unknown creature in Africa, after all. And in 1856, an American explorer in Africa shot one of the creatures and skinned it. He brought the furry skin

Dr. Dian Fossey spent many years studying gorillas. She found that they are gentle creatures that eat mainly fruits and plants, and are not really dangerous to people.

to Europe for scientists to see. So, the mysterious huge, furry, humanlike monster that most scientists had thought was either a legend or a made-up story turned out to be real. It was, of course, the animal that we now call a gorilla!

For a long time, people believed that gorillas were fierce, savage creatures that might kill any human they encountered. Today we know they are gentle animals that eat mainly fruits and vegetables.

The Legend That Became a Fact

One of the world's oldest stories is the story of the Trojan War. In this war, ancient Greece defeated the city of Troy, which was on the coast of what is now Turkey. Ancient legends, poems, and plays tell marvelous and fantastic tales of this war.

The stories tell how, more than three thousand years ago, a Greek army sailed across the Aegean Sea to attack Troy. There were terrible battles as the Greeks tried to break into the city. Brave

heroes on both sides challenged one another and fought to the death. Because gods and goddesses sometimes helped one side or the other, many strange and magical events took place. But the war dragged on for ten years, with no sign that it would ever end.

Then, one morning, the people of Troy awoke to find that the Greeks had apparently given up and sailed away. But they had left behind a huge wooden horse. A Greek prisoner told the Trojans that the horse was sacred and would bring the protection of the gods. So the Trojans dragged the statue into the city. Then they began to feast and make merry to celebrate their victory.

Late that night while the city slept, a hidden door in the statue opened up. A group of Greek soldiers climbed out, rushed to the city gate, and opened it. The Greek army had only pretended to sail away. Now it had come back under cover of darkness. The Greeks stormed into the city, taking it by surprise. They massacred the Trojan soldiers, rounded up the people to be carried off as slaves, and burned Troy to the ground.

One of the greatest tales of the Trojan War is the *Iliad*, meaning "story of Ilium." (Ilium was the Greek name for Troy.) According to tradition, a Greek poet named Homer wrote the *Iliad* more than 2,700 years ago. During the centuries since then, millions of people have read the *Iliad*. It is regarded as one of the world's greatest epics, or story-poems.

Long ago, many people believed the story of the Trojan War as told in the *Iliad* and other books was true. But as time went on, people came to feel it was only a legend. It contained too many fantastic happenings to be true. Besides, there were no ruins of any city known as Ilium or Troy, as there were of many other ancient cities. Most historians doubted that such a place ever existed.

But a few people thought that the Trojan War did take place. They believed that there had been a city of Troy that the Greeks had captured and destroyed as Homer and others said. There were several places where Troy might have stood. One of these was a high mound of earth known as Hissarlik, on the coast of Turkey. A few people thought the ruins of Troy might lie buried within this mound.

And so, by the mid-1800's, the Trojan War had become something that people talked about and argued over. Was it only a legend, or had it really happened? Were the ruins of Troy actually buried somewhere, such as beneath the mound of Hissarlik?

One person who thought so was a wealthy German-born businessman named Heinrich Schliemann (HYN rihk SHLEE mahn). He had read the *Iliad* over and over. It seemed to him that Hissarlik was very much like the land Homer had described as being around Troy. Schliemann became convinced that he could find the ruins of Troy by digging in Hissarlik. In 1870, when he was forty-eight years old, Schliemann and his wife, Sophia, moved to Turkey and hired workmen to begin digging.

Nearly all historians, scientists, and most other people thought Schliemann was foolish. They felt he was trying to prove that a fairy tale was true. They thought it would be a waste of time to dig up Hissarlik. But Schliemann didn't care in the least what anyone else thought. He was sure he would find Troy.

These ruins are part of the walls that once surrounded two of the nine ancient cities found on the site of Troy.

Convinced that Troy lay at the bottom of the mound, Schliemann had his workmen dig a huge trench. It soon became clear that the mound contained the remains of not only one city, but a number of cities, built one on top of the other! Was one of them Troy? And if so, which one?

The digging went on for three years. Altogether, the ruins of nine cities were uncovered. But there was no sign that any of these ruins had been the rich and powerful city Homer had described.

Schliemann decided to give up. But on the day before he was to leave Turkey, a miracle happened. Looking at the stone ruins for the last time, his eye caught a gleam of metal. He began to dig among the stones with a large knife—and he uncovered a tremendous treasure!

In one large silver vase alone, he found two gold crowns, six gold bracelets, two small gold goblets, sixty gold earrings, thousands of small gold rings, and many other objects of gold and silver. Schliemann believed that someone had hidden this treasure under the wall thousands of years before, when the city was attacked. Furthermore, the stone wall under which he found all this wealth was scorched and blackened as if by a terrible fire. Schliemann felt this wall must have been part of the city that the Greeks had burned. He was now sure that he had, indeed, found Troy. He had proved that it was a real place and not a legend!

This is Sophia Schliemann, wearing some of the ancient jewelry her husband found at Troy.

Archaeologists (ahr kee AHL uh jihsts)—scientists who study ancient times and places—continued Schliemann's work at Hissarlik. One of the nine cities was indeed Homer's Troy, but archaeologists are not certain which one. Schliemann found the treasure in the second city from the bottom, which he declared was Homer's Troy. Today, however, scholars believe that the seventh city from the bottom was probably Homer's Troy.

However, Schliemann did solve the mystery and prove that Troy was a real place, not just part of a legend. Most historians and archaeologists now believe that many legends are based, at least partly, on real events and places.

What's Mysterious About a Mummy?

To many people, the mummies of ancient Egypt are mysterious and a bit frightening. These people wonder why the ancient Egyptians preserved dead bodies and how they were able to do so. Did the ancient Egyptians have a secret way of doing this, a way we no longer know?

Actually, there's nothing mysterious about mummies. Scientists who study the ancient Egyptians know exactly how and why they preserved their dead people.

It was simply part of the ancient Egyptian religion to keep dead people well preserved. The Egyptians believed in life after death, but they also believed that people used the same bodies in the

afterlife that they had when they were alive. So, when an Egyptian died, his or her family and friends tried to have the body preserved as well as possible, so as to be used again. They had it made into a mummy.

The Egyptians probably learned mummy-making by accident. At first, they just buried the bodies of dead people in shallow holes in the sand at the edge of the desert. The hot, dry sand preserved a body somewhat, drying it out so that it didn't just rot away as dead things usually do. The Egyptians discovered this, and began trying to deliberately preserve the bodies of dead people by drying them out and carefully wrapping them up.

After a time, Egyptian undertakers discovered a salty kind of chemical that dried a body out even better than sand. They would pack the body of a dead person in some of this chemical until the body was completely dried. Then, around and around the body they wrapped strips of cloth soaked in a kind of glue. After that, they put the mummy into a coffin and sealed it away in a tomb, or—if the person had been very important—a secret room in a pyramid. The process—from death to burial—took about seventy days.

Scientists have learned a great deal about the people of ancient Egypt and their way of life by examining mummies.

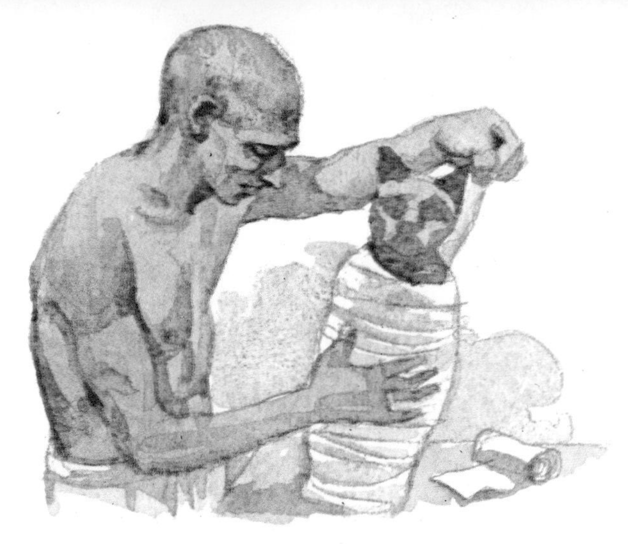

However, the ancient Egyptians didn't make mummies only of people. They often had mummies made of dead pets they were fond of—cats, birds, and even crocodiles!

An Egyptian tomb, especially one for a rich person, was underground and always sealed up tight. The heat and dryness in the tomb helped preserve the mummy as well as the other things that had been put into the tomb. Thus, many of the mummies that have been found and unwrapped show us what the dead person looked like when he or she was alive.

But even more important than that, a well-preserved mummy can tell scientists a great many things about what life was like in ancient Egypt. For example, from examining mummies, scientists have found that many ancient Egyptians probably coughed a lot—their lungs were damaged from constantly breathing in tiny grains of desert sand that blew about in the air. Many ancient Egyptians were sickly because of parasites—tiny worms that lived inside their bodies and caused them to have fevers and aches. The teeth of some pharaohs (kings) were so bad that these men, rich and powerful though they were, must have often suffered from dreadful toothaches!

Scientists have even been able to take fingerprints and toeprints from the well-preserved skin of some mummies. Such prints can show whether the mummy was once a wealthy person who wore sandals and did little work, or a poor person who went barefoot and worked hard enough to get calluses on his or her fingers.

The cloth wrappings around a mummy's body also help preserve some of the things people wore. Jewelry, sandals, and other things, as good as new, have been found inside many mummy wrappings.

So, there's really nothing mysterious or frightening about how mummies are preserved. The "secret" is mostly just Egypt's hot, dry weather and the drying chemical the Egyptians discovered. But it's lucky for us that many mummies are so well preserved. They have helped us learn and understand a lot about the people of ancient Egypt and their ways of life.

The Search for the Source of the Nile

The Nile River flows for 4,145 miles (6,671 kilometers) through northeast Africa. It is the world's longest river. It is also a very important river. Without its water to irrigate the land so that crops can grow, Egypt could never have existed.

This map, made in 1486, was based on a map Ptolemy drew some thirteen hundred years earlier. It shows the "Mountains of the Moon" as the source of the Nile, just as Ptolemy did.

Yet, for thousands of years, the source, or beginning, of this mighty river was a mystery. No one knew where this vast flow of water came from!

About 2,400 years ago, a Greek named Herodotus (huh RAHD uh tuhs), who was curious about things, tried to follow the Nile to its beginning. He traveled as far as present-day Aswan, Egypt, but there he had to stop. He had heard reports that farther to the south the Nile flowed through the country of Kush (now called Sudan), but he was unable to go on.

Some 1,800 years ago, the Greek scientist Ptolemy (TAHL uh mee), who lived in Egypt, wrote some geography books. In one of these books he said that the Nile came from water that flowed out of two huge lakes in the middle of Africa. He also said that streams flowing from a range of mountains he called the "Mountains of the Moon" formed these lakes. So, according to Ptolemy, the source of the Nile was thousands of miles (km) from Egypt.

For nearly 1,500 years, Ptolemy's book provided the only information about the source of the Nile. No Europeans could get into Africa during that time to find out if Ptolemy was right. The Turkish Empire, which was usually at war with most of Europe, blocked the way. But then, in the 1600's, the Turkish Empire became very weak. Missionaries and adventurers from Europe began flocking to Africa.

They quickly found out that no one had yet found the source of the Nile. Many Africans didn't know if the lakes and mountains Ptolemy had written about even existed. Some thought that the source of the Nile was in the mountains of the country of Ethiopia, to the south. But no one was sure.

A number of Europeans became excited by the idea of looking for the source of the Nile. One of the first to try was a Scotsman named James Bruce. He lived for a time in Egypt and learned to speak Arabic, a common language of North Africa. Then, in the year 1768, he took a boat from the city of Cairo and started up the Nile. He thought he could just follow the river up into central Ethiopia until he came to its source.

But when Bruce neared the Egyptian city of Aswan he ran into warring tribes. It was too dangerous to keep going up the river, so Bruce left the boat and traveled across the desert to the Red Sea. There, he found a boat that took him to a town on the coast of Ethiopia. It took him three months to get from that town to the middle of the country.

Bruce found some guides who spoke Arabic. He told them he wanted to find the source of the great river that flowed into Egypt. They took him into the mountains to a place where a tiny spring bubbled out of the ground and sent its waters trickling down the mountainside. Other trickles of water joined it, until it finally became a mighty stream that flowed toward Egypt.

Sure that he had found the source of the Nile, James Bruce started home. But he had a very difficult time. He nearly died crossing a desert on foot. And, as happened to many European explorers in Africa, he caught a disease that made him very sick. Even worse, when he finally did get back to England, no one believed that he had really been to Ethiopia! Not until 1790, when he published a book about his travels, did people believe him.

James Bruce thought he would go down in history as the man who, after thousands of years, discovered the true source of the Nile. But, as it turned out, he hadn't found the main source at all. The spring he found is actually the source of *another* river. This river, now known as the Blue Nile, flows into the Nile before the Nile reaches Egypt.

More explorers, as well as missionaries, now began going to Africa. Before long, some of them

realized that the true source of the Nile hadn't been found. They discovered that the main branch of the Nile, now known as the White Nile, went on far past Ethiopia. Its source had to be closer to the middle of Africa, just as Ptolemy had said.

In 1839, a Turkish army officer named Selim Bimbashi set out with several sailboats to find the source of the Nile. He tried again in 1841 and 1842, but was never able to get past Sudan. Rapids stopped the boats.

Between 1846 and 1849, two German missionaries, Johann Krapf and Johann Rebmann, managed to get farther into the center of Africa than any other European yet had. Each of them, exploring separately, saw snow-covered mountains that had never been mapped. And Krapf heard tales of a great shining sea that lay in the center of the land, beyond two mountains that were always capped with snow. Krapf and Rebmann told each other what they had seen and heard. They wondered if the "sea" might actually be one of the huge lakes that Ptolemy had written about. And perhaps the two mountains were some of the "Mountains of the Moon."

The two men carefully drew a map based on the tales, showing the sea and mountains, and sent it back to Europe. Some people thought the map was nonsense. But the British Royal Geographical Society decided there might be something to it. They raised the money to send an expedition to Africa to look for the great inland sea. To head the expedition, they picked a man named Richard Burton.

Burton was a famous explorer. He had lived in North Africa for a number of years and learned to speak Arabic perfectly. In fact, he translated a number of old, old Arabic tales into English. These stories make up the famous children's book *The Arabian Nights*. For years, Burton had wanted to search for the source of the Nile. Now his chance had come.

With the money provided, Burton bought many donkeys to carry heavy supplies and hired more than a hundred Africans to carry lighter things. On

June 16, 1857, the expedition started out. With Burton was an army officer named John Speke, who was a close friend.

They headed straight in toward the center of Africa, making their way through thick forests and across flooded rivers and swamps. Both Burton and Speke came down with serious ear infections and became almost deaf. Many of the Africans began to leave the expedition, and a number of the donkeys died. Food ran short. Burton and Speke were so sick that Burton could not walk and Speke became almost blind. They had to be carried.

Ten months after it had started out, the expedition reached the shore of what seemed to be a great inland sea. Burton and Speke thought they had found what they were looking for, but their hopes were soon dashed. Africans who lived by the lake showed them that no river flowed out of it. Burton and Speke had discovered the big lake that is now called Lake Tanganyika (TAN guhn YEE kuh), but it was not the source of the Nile.

However, Africans told the two Englishmen of another big lake only two weeks' journey away. Burton was too sick to go any farther, so Speke, who could now see again, went to find out if the tale were true.

What Speke found was an enormous lake that did, indeed, look like a sea. He was the first European to see this lake. He named it Lake

Lake Victoria, the largest lake in Africa, is named for Queen Victoria. The one stream that runs out of this lake is the beginning of the Nile River.

Victoria, after the woman who was then queen of Great Britain. This lake is the largest lake in Africa and the second largest freshwater lake in the world. (Only Lake Superior, between the United States and Canada, is larger.)

Speke was sure that Lake Victoria was the main source of the Nile, and he was right. However, it took several more explorers and many more years to prove this. It wasn't until 1875 that a famous explorer named Henry Stanley found that only one stream runs out of Lake Victoria. That stream is, indeed, the beginning of the Nile. Thus Stanley finally solved the mystery of the Nile's source and showed that Ptolemy had been almost right.

More than ten years later, in 1889, Stanley also discovered that Ptolemy had been very nearly right about the "Mountains of the Moon." Stanley found that they are a range of mountains not far beyond Lake Victoria. Today, these mountains are known as the Ruwenzori (ROO wehn ZOOR ee) Range. Melting snows from these mountains feed some of the farthest streams that flow into the Nile. But these streams are not the source of the Nile.

The search for the source of the Nile was of great importance. It did far more than just show where a river begins. All the explorers who searched for the source of the Nile helped to open up the mysterious, hidden parts of Africa, and show the world what is there.

The Canals of Mars

A hundred years ago, the only way astronomers could learn about other planets was to use a telescope. Astronomers spent hours on end staring through telescopes at a particular planet, trying to make out as much as they could of the faint, blurry object they saw.

Because Mars is one of the closest planets to Earth, astronomers often studied it. To the naked eye, Mars appeared reddish, but through a telescope, it looked like an orange ball with patches of white at its north and south poles. Astronomers were sure those white patches were masses of ice or snow. But there wasn't much else they could make out.

In 1877, an Italian astronomer, Giovanni Schiaparelli, spent a great deal of time studying Mars. Schiaparelli was sure he could see something that, apparently, no one else had seen—a number of long, dark lines on the face of Mars. These lines ran in different directions, crisscrossing one another in places. Sometimes he could barely see them and sometimes he couldn't see them at all, but at times they seemed strong and clear.

Schiaparelli thought the lines were probably natural formations of some sort, such as dry riverbeds. When he wrote a report about them, he called them *canali*, Italian for *channels*. But *canali* also means *canals*. When his report was translated into English, *canali* became *canals*.

Now a canal is very different from a channel. Channels usually form naturally, but a canal isn't a natural formation. It's a long, narrow waterway that people dig to make water flow from one place to another, for boats to travel on, or to bring water to farmland. Thus, if there were canals on Mars, intelligent living creatures—Martians—must have made them.

So, the idea that intelligent creatures of some sort lived on Mars, or had once lived there, became popular. Not only did many ordinary people believe it, but so did a great many scientists. One famous American scientist even figured out why Martians might need so many canals. He thought it was because Mars was probably a desert world. The Martians, he said, had dug the canals to bring water to their cities from the huge piles of snow at the north and south poles.

However, while a number of astronomers thought they could see lines on Mars, there were many who couldn't—and who didn't think there really were any. So, an argument began between people who thought there were canals on Mars, and those who thought there weren't.

The argument went on for nearly ninety years. Then space flight began and scientists had a way to find out for sure. They could send "robot" spacecraft to Mars to take pictures. The pictures, when radioed back to Earth, would show if Mars had canals.

When the spacecraft *Mariner 4* was launched on its trip to Mars in 1964, there was a good deal of excitement. Those who believed in the canals wondered if they would turn out to be natural formations, as Schiaparelli had thought, or actual canals. Would they turn out to be ages old—dug long, long ago, by creatures that were now extinct? Or, would the pictures show that even now there were intelligent living beings on Mars?

The pictures that *Mariner 4* sent back surprised most scientists and other interested people. The pictures showed that Mars was rocky and dotted with craters, like the moon. No canals showed on any of the pictures. Those who had hoped to see canals were disappointed, of course. But the pictures showed only a tiny, tiny piece of Mars. These people were sure that more pictures, showing more of the planet, would be sure to have at least one canal on them.

In 1969, two more Mariners flew around Mars. They sent back two hundred pictures of a fair-sized portion of the planet. These pictures showed rocky mountains and desert valleys, but still no sign of canals. And the people who had hoped for canals began to get worried!

By 1972, the matter was settled once and for all. The spacecraft *Mariner 9* sent back more than seven thousand pictures of the surface of Mars.

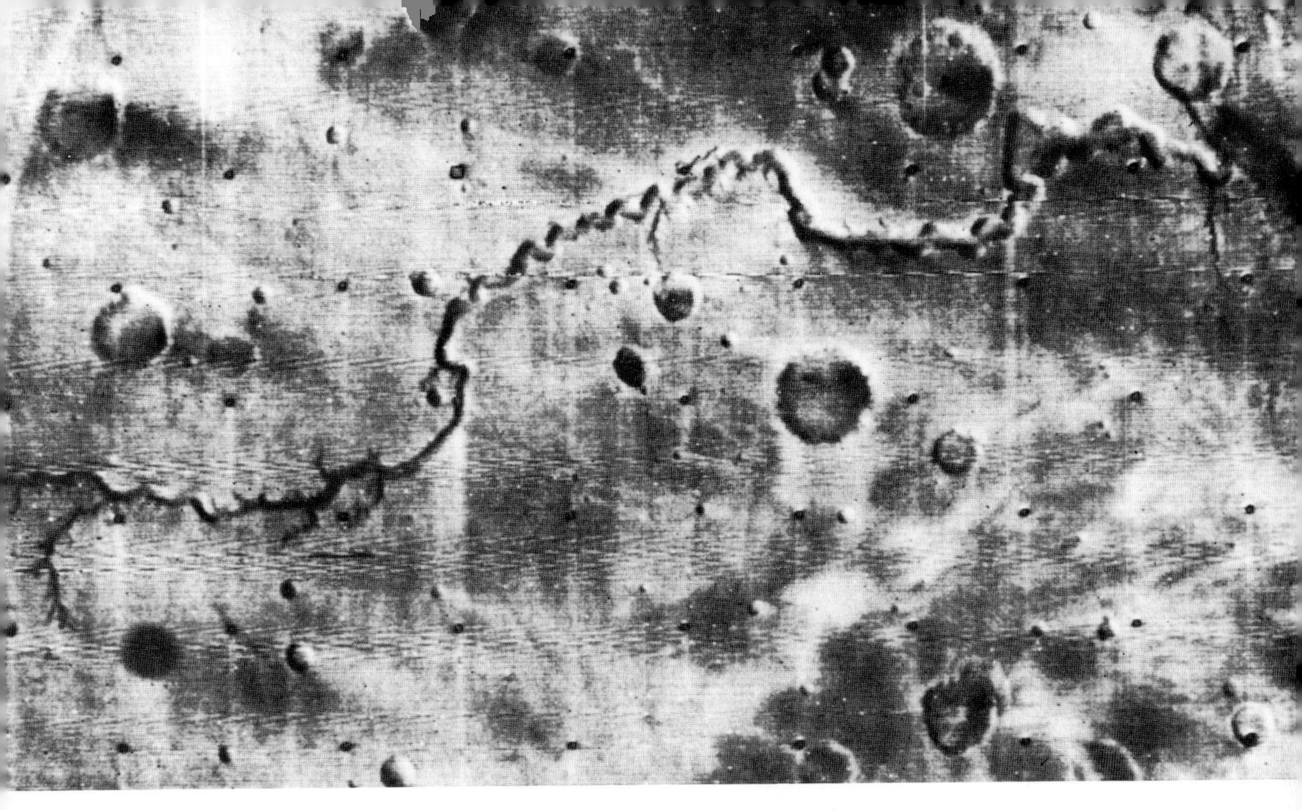

This photograph of a section of Mars, taken by Mariner 9, shows what seems to be a dry riverbed or channel. Of the thousands of photographs taken, not one shows any canals.

The pictures showed that Mars is a rocky, desert world of mountains, valleys, old volcanoes, craters, and an enormous canyon. The pictures also showed what look like channels or dry riverbeds. It seems, then, that Mars does have channels—but not canals.

Most scientists now feel that Schiaparelli and the others who saw lines on Mars were simply tricked by their own eyes. Because of this, for nearly a hundred years people wondered about the Martian canals, books were written about them, and scientists argued over them—and they were never there at all!

Tales of Man-Eating Trees!

Until thirty or forty years ago, many parts of Africa, Asia, and South America still had not been very well explored. Many people thought that strange, unknown things might live in these unexplored areas. And one of the strangest things that supposedly lived in some of those places was—trees that ate people!

The first tales of man-eating trees came out in the year 1783. A doctor wrote a magazine article about such tales that he had heard in Southeast Asia, in what is now the country of Malaysia. According to the tales, the trees grew in the Malaysian jungles and looked like ordinary trees. But if some unsuspecting person walked too close to one, it would reach out with its branches and

Escaped from the Embrace of the Man-Eating Tree

Mr. W. C. Bryant, Exploring in the Island Jungle of the Philippines, Tells of the Hungry Grasping Arms and Hissing Leaves of the Cannibal Tree Which Strained to Reach Him

Natives of Mindanao, Philippine Islands, Beating Musical Instruments to Drive Away Ghosts and Devils.

Seemed Horribly Alive and Alert, and from All Directions the Tentacled ... Reached for Him and He Saw in the Deadly Circle Around the Trunk the Skulls and Bones of Its Unfortunate Victims.

Photograph of a Part of Mr. Bryant's Exploring Expedition, Showing One of the Native Water Buffalo.

Tales of trees that ate people were common in the 1920's and 1930's, as shown by this page from a 1925 newspaper. But no one has ever found such trees.

seize him! The doctor wrote that the people worshiped some of the trees as gods, and even sacrificed people to them!

After that, stories of trees that ate people began to come out of other parts of Asia, as well as Africa and South America. Here was another mystery for people to wonder about. Could there really be such a thing as trees that ate humans? As is always the case, some people believed the stories and some did not.

Even in the 1930's, some newspapers printed stories about trees that ate people. The trees were supposed to be in a swampy jungle region in the South American country of Paraguay. It was said that the trees drew people to them with the sweet smell of their flowers. When someone got close enough, some of the tree's huge leaves would suddenly wrap themselves around the person, who would then be helpless.

Scientists knew such tales just weren't true. And during the last forty years or so, most of the last of the jungles and swamps of Asia, Africa, and South America have been explored. Nobody ever found any people-eating trees. Today, we no longer hear tales of such things.

But some people will always believe that in wild, hidden-away places there are such things as monsters or man-eating trees.

The Mystery of the Wintry Summer

June is a warm month in the United States and most of Canada. Trees and bushes wear pale new leaves, the grass is green, and the birds, gone all winter, have come back. In early June, people look forward to a long, pleasant summer.

But in early June 1816, many people wondered if there was going to *be* a summer! In that year, June started acting more like a winter month than a summer one.

At first it seemed as if summer had come early. On the fourth of June, the temperature in much of New England and southeastern Canada was a sizzling 90° Fahrenheit (32° Celsius) or more. Then the temperature began to drop. And it kept right on dropping for the next twenty-four hours. The air went from warm to cool to cold to freezing! On the nights of June 5 and 6, there was frost from southeastern Canada down to the state of Virginia. In some places, creeks and streams had ice an inch (2.5 centimeters) thick.

Then, on the night of June 7 and the morning of June 8, a howling storm dumped sleet and snow on all the New England States as well as New York state and Ohio. In some parts of New England, snowdrifts were twenty inches (51 cm) high.

The strange, wintry weather continued for several days. Then the temperature began to rise. People sighed with relief. They were glad that the freak spell of cold was over. But by this time, the cold had killed the new leaves on trees. And the sprouts of corn and garden vegetables that had just poked up out of the ground were dead. Farmers planted new crops.

But the wintry weather hadn't gone away for good. On July 5, it came roaring back with a freezing storm. In Canada, lakes, ponds, and streams froze over. It wasn't until nearly the middle of the month that the weather warmed up again.

By now a lot of people were in trouble. The second attack of winter had killed much of the second corn crop farmers had planted. In Canada, much of the wheat crop was ruined, too. There was a shortage of food.

Then the cold weather struck again! On August 21, a day that's often blisteringly hot, there was a frost in Canada and the northern New England States. More corn and wheat were destroyed, and many crops of vegetables, as well. And on August 30, there was still another frost!

Canada and the northern part of the United States weren't the only places struck by these strange attacks of wintry weather. That year, many parts of the world experienced low temperatures, frosts, and ruined crops. The extreme cold may have hit other parts of North America, too. But the American Indians—the only ones then living in certain parts of the continent—did not keep records of such things, so we don't know for sure.

People who lived through that wintry summer of 1816 told tales of it all their lives. Most of them

simply thought of it as a freak thing that had never happened before and would probably never happen again.

But there was a mystery about all this cold, snowy weather during what should have been hot, summer months. *Why* had this happened? Why did the entire world experience temperatures lower than normal that summer? At the time, no one knew why. But now, scientists think they have the answer.

In the spring of 1815, Mount Tambora, a volcano on an island in Southeast Asia, erupted. The tremendous eruption released six million times more energy than an atomic bomb! More than four thousand feet (1,220 meters) of the top of the volcano blew into the sky as fine dust. The eruption also hurled tons and tons of ash into the air.

Carried high into the air, this mixture of dust and ash slowly spread out, forming a dark cloud over the whole world. This cloud caused the cold weather. Some of the sunlight that would have reached the earth was stopped by the cloud and reflected back out into space. Thus, the earth did not get as warm that summer as it should have.

In time, rain and snow carried the particles of dust and ash back down to earth, and the cloud thinned out and vanished. The weather returned to normal. There have been many other volcanic eruptions since then, and some of them, too, affected the weather. But no other eruption has ever put as much dust and ash into the air as did the eruption of Mount Tambora in 1815. So we have never had another summer as wintry as that of 1816.

Island of Mysteries

On Easter Sunday in 1722, the men of a Dutch ship sailing in the South Pacific Ocean sighted a tiny, unknown island. They landed to explore the place—and found a mystery. In time, the island would become known as the "island of a thousand mysteries."

What the Dutch explorers found on the island were hundreds of huge, gray-black stone statues. Some were more than thirty feet (9 meters) high and weighed as much as ninety tons (82 metric tons). Each statue was the same—the head and upper body of a man with long ears, thin lips, deep-set eyes, and a long, straight nose. Sometimes a strange sort of "hat" made of red stone was on the head.

To the Dutch, the people living on the island seemed like savages. They wore no clothes, had few tools, and lived in crude huts. Surely these people could not have made the huge statues and set them up all over the island. But then, who had?

The captain of the ship named the place Easter Island, because of the day on which he discovered it. During the next hundred years a number of other explorers from various European countries visited Easter Island. They, too, marveled at the giant stone statues.

In 1864, a French missionary arrived at Easter Island. He found that almost all the statues had been pulled down! Many of them lay broken on the ground, and others were half buried in piles of stones. Furthermore, although the first explorers had reported that about four thousand people lived on the island, there were now only about six hundred! What had happened?

There was another mystery on the island, too. A few of the people had some old wooden boards covered with what seemed to be a kind of picture writing. None of the people on any of the many other islands in the Pacific Ocean had ever invented writing, but it certainly looked as if someone on Easter Island had. Yet, it didn't seem possible that the primitive people living there had done it.

And so, Easter Island now abounded in mysteries. Who had carved the statues? Why had they been carved? Why had they been destroyed? What had become of all the people? Who had invented the writing?

In recent years, scientists have managed to work out most of the strange story of Easter Island. Here is what they found.

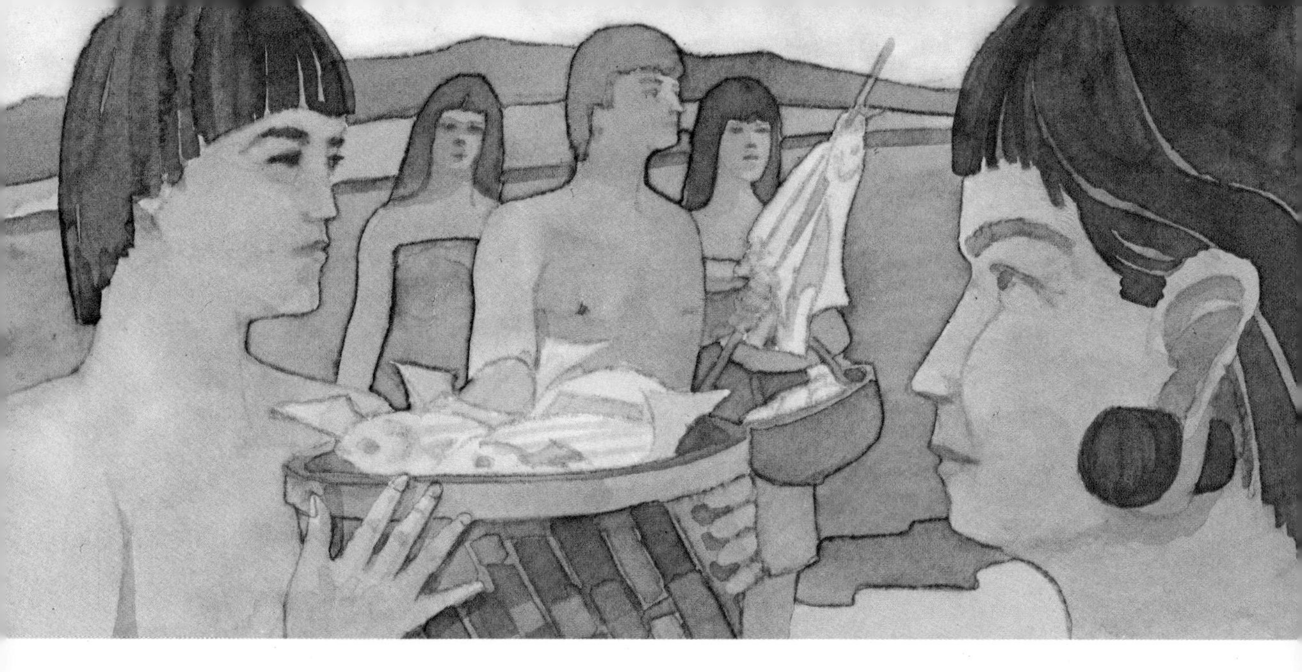

About six hundred years ago, Easter Island was shared by two groups of people. These two groups had evidently come from two different places. One group was probably Polynesian. They were tall, light-skinned, and wavy-haired, like many of the people of Hawaii. The other group may have been South American Indians from Peru.

One group decorated themselves in an unusual way. They pierced their ears and put wooden plugs into the holes to make them bigger and stretch the ears out. So, one group of people had long ears, and the other group had ordinary short ears.

The Long-Ears had a custom of burying the bones of their ancestors beneath platforms of stone. They then put huge stone statues up on the platforms. The statues represented their ancestors. The Long-Ears believed that a statue had the power to protect the family group who had put it up.

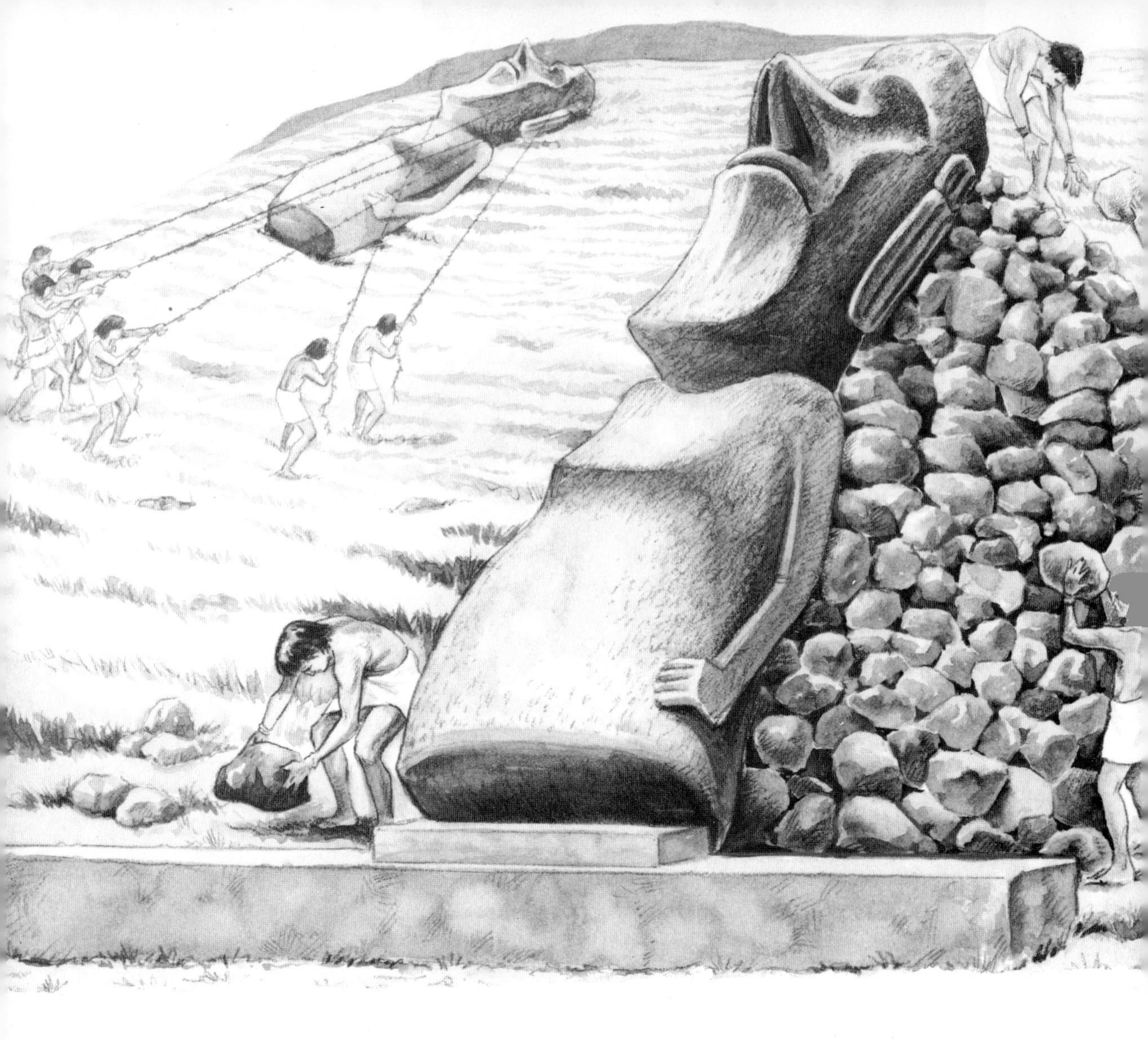

The statues were carved out of the side of a volcano that rises over the island. The rock forming the volcano is soft, and the people used sharp stone tools to do the carving. When a statue was finished, many people using vine ropes dragged it to its platform. They raised it by piling rocks and dirt under the head, little by little, which lifted it slowly upward on an angle. When it was standing

By about 1840, most of the Easter Island statues were partly buried or had been toppled over.

Today, some of the statues have been set up again, so that they look much as they did hundreds of years ago.

up straight on the platform, the rocks and dirt were taken away.

In time, the Short-Ears also began making statues. Perhaps they were forced to, for the Long-Ears apparently ruled the island. Or perhaps the two groups came to honor their ancestors in the same way. At any rate, making the statues seemed to become the most important thing in the world to the Easter Islanders. They spent more and more time on their carving. Altogether, they made about a thousand statues over several hundred years.

Then a war broke out between the two groups. Perhaps the Short-Ears grew tired of being ruled by the Long-Ears. In any event, the Short-Ears killed almost all the Long-Ears! After that, many family groups fought with each other. The fighting lasted for years, and no more statues were ever made.

The groups were fighting each other when the Dutch sailors arrived. And during the next hundred years there was continual killing, starvation, and terror! We still don't know why the people pulled down the statues and destroyed them during this time. One guess is that the people realized the statues had no power to protect them, so they destroyed the statues in anger.

To make things even worse, some of the ships that came to the island took many of the people away as slaves. The few who came back brought

A number of wooden tablets found on Easter Island have a kind of picture writing carved on them. But no one can now read this writing.

sickness to the island, and many of the people died. All this was why so few people were finally left.

Thus most of the mysteries of Easter Island have been solved. But there is still at least one left. No one can now read the writing invented by the Easter Islanders of long ago. We may never know what the writing on the wooden boards means.

Things are much better for the Easter Islanders today. There are now about two thousand of them, and their island is making money from tourists. Some of the great stone statues have been raised up again. Tourists now come to stare at them in wonder, just as the Dutch sailors did when they first saw them more than 250 years ago.

Books to Read

There are many good books about the mysteries, wonders, and fantasies that have puzzled and fascinated people for centuries. A few are listed here. Your school or public library will have some of these, as well as many others.

Ages 5 to 8

Is There Life in Outer Space? by Franklyn M. Branley (Crowell, 1984)
Simply but effectively written by a professional astronomer, this book can be read aloud to preschoolers and also enjoyed by early readers. It describes the investigations of the solar system's planets and discusses what kind of life most probably exists on other planets in other galaxies.

Monsters of North America by William Wise (Putnam, 1978)
This book describes some of the many strange monsters that have been reported in the United States and Canada, such as the Missouri Monster, the Piasa birds, and Bigfoot. The author makes it plain that there is little or no evidence for most of these creatures.

Secrets of the Mummies by Joyce Milton (Random House, 1984)
A simply-presented discussion of facts about mummies and mummification that mixes in information about ancient Egypt, the discoveries of tombs containing royal mummies, and the work of archaeologists.

UFO's by Susan Harris (Watts, 1980)
A number of case histories of UFO sightings are described, and the author explains some of the many things that have been mistaken for UFO's. A list of things to do is provided for anyone who thinks they have seen a UFO, in order to determine whether the sighting is genuine or a mistake.

Ages 9 to 12

The Book of the Unknown by Harold and Genevieve Woods (Random House, 1982)
Up-to-date information about many different mysteries, such as ESP, Stonehenge, Black Holes, etc.

Close Encounters: A Factual Report on UFO's by Sherman Larsen (Raintree, 1978)
A scientific examination of the mystery of UFO's, which does not attempt to offer an answer, but simply presents facts.

Cosmic Quest: Searching for Intelligent Life Among the Stars by Margaret Poynter and Michael Klein (Atheneum, 1984)
The authors present a picture of the universe as it is currently understood, with an explanation of how life might have emerged on other planets and how we are going about trying to make contact with other intelligent living creatures in space.

Dinosaurs, Asteroids, and Superstars: Why the Dinosaurs Disappeared by Franklyn M. Branley (Crowell, 1982)
The author first explains how scientists are able to date and describe things

from fossil remains, and then discusses all the various theories of dinosaur extinction.

Henry Stanley and the Quest for the Source of the Nile by Daniel Cohen (Dutton, 1985)
Here is the exciting story of the man who found the source of the Nile.

How Did We Find Out About Black Holes? by Isaac Asimov (Walker, 1978)
A careful explanation of how astronomers observe and analyze unusual behavior of stars, and how certain stars may (theoretically) change into black holes.

Monsters from Outer Space by William Wise (Putnam, 1979)
An explanation of the many ways people can be fooled into thinking they have seen a UFO.

Mummies Made in Egypt by Aliki (Crowell, 1979)
A lavishly illustrated book that explains the process used by the Egyptians to mummify a body.

The Mystery of Stonehenge by Franklyn M. Branley (Harper, 1969)
This book provides the known facts about the building of Stonehenge and offers theories about why it was built and how it was used.

The Mystery of the Loch Ness Monster by Jeanne Bendick (McGraw-Hill, 1976)
A thorough presentation of all the known facts, from information about the lake itself to a record of everything that has been done to find out whether there actually is some unusual living thing in it.

Science Looks at Mysterious Monsters by Thomas Aylesworth (Messner, 1982)
This book offers a sober appraisal of all the evidence, for and against, a number of well-known modern "monsters"—Bigfoot, the Loch Ness monster, and others. The reader can decide for himself or herself, based on the facts, whether each creature actually exists.

Strange Mysteries from around the World by Seymour Simon (Four Winds, 1980)
A collection of many odd mysteries, from "rains" of fish and frogs to UFO's. The author is careful to separate positive facts from unsubstantiated claims.

Those Mysterious UFO's: The Story of Unidentified Flying Objects by David Knight (Parents, 1975)
A history of eighty years of UFO sightings is covered, together with a discussion of the various investigations that were made.

What Really Happened to the Dinosaurs? by Daniel Cohen (Dutton, 1977)
A very clearly presented look at most of the many ideas about what caused dinosaurs to become extinct, including the idea that they are *not* extinct, but still fill the world as the creatures we call birds.

New Words

Here are some of the words you have met in this book. Many of them may be new to you. All are useful words to know. Next to each word, you'll see how to say the word: **abominable** (uh BAHM uh nuh buhl). The part in capital letters is said more loudly than the rest of the word. One or two sentences tell what the word means.

abominable (uh BAHM uh nuh buhl)
Abominable means something that is very disgusting or hateful.

atmosphere (AT muh sfihr)
An atmosphere is a gas or mixture of gases surrounding a planet. Earth's air is its atmosphere.

billion (BIHL yuhn)
A billion is one thousand millions in the U.S. and Canada. In Great Britain, a billion is one million millions.

biochemist (by oh KEHM ihst)
A biochemist is a scientist who deals with the chemical processes of living animals and plants.

camouflage (KAM uh flahzh)
To camouflage means to disguise something in order to hide it. An animal's coloring often blends into its surroundings, so that it is very hard to see.

ceremony (SEHR uh moh nee)
A ceremony is a way of doing things at a special occasion such as a wedding or funeral.

constellation (kahn stuh LAY shuhn)
A constellation is a group of stars that appear to form a special shape or pattern.

crevice (KREHV ihs)
A crevice is a narrow split or crack.

disk (dihsk)
A disk is a thin, flat, round object such as a coin.

evidence (EHV uh duhns)
Evidence is anything that shows or makes clear what is true or what is not true.

expedition (ehks puh DIHSH uhn)
An expedition is a journey for a special purpose, such as to search for something. It is also the group making such a journey.

fantasy (FAN tuh see)
A fantasy is something that is not real, something that exists only in the imagination. Books such as *Alice's Adventures in Wonderland* and *Charlotte's Web* are fantasies.

fossil (FAHS uhl)
A fossil is the hardened remains or trace of an animal or plant that lived long ago.

Himalaya (hih muh LAY uh)
The Himalaya (or Himalayas) is the world's highest mountain range. It lies between India and China.

hoax (hohks)
A hoax is a trick or a made-up story that tries to make people believe something is true when it is not.

humid (HYOO mihd)
Humid means moist or damp.

irrigate (IHR uh gayt)
To irrigate is to supply land with water.

meteor (MEE tee uhr)
A meteor is a chunk of stone or metal from space that has entered Earth's atmosphere and is burning up as it falls to the ground. Meteors are often called falling stars or shooting stars.

meteorite (MEE tee uh ryt)
A meteorite is a meteor that has reached the ground before burning up.

meteoroid (MEE tee uh roihd)
A meteoroid is a chunk of rock or metal that is moving through space in orbit around the sun.

methane (MEHTH ayn)
Methane is a colorless, odorless gas that will burn. If a gas is made cold enough, it becomes a liquid. On Saturn's moon Titan, there may be lakes of liquid methane.

nitrogen (NY truh juhn)
Nitrogen is a colorless, odorless gas. It makes up about 78 per cent of Earth's atmosphere and nearly all of the atmosphere of Titan.

Norse (nawrs)
The Norse were the people of ancient Scandinavia, which includes the modern nations of Norway, Sweden, and Denmark.

nuclear (NOO klee uhr)
Nuclear means having to do with atomic energy.

permanent (PUR muh nuhnt)
Permanent means lasting.

primitive (PRIHM uh tihv)
Primitive means of prehistoric times, or something that is like the things of prehistoric times. Primitive people are like prehistoric people.

process (PRAHS ehs)
A process is a series of actions that are taken in order to do a complete job of something.

Pygmy (PIHG mee)
A Pygmy (capital "P") is any one of a group of African people who are quite short. The word *pygmy* (small "p") is a general term for anything small.

radar (RAY dahr)
Radar is an instrument for finding the distance, direction, and speed of unseen objects by the reflection of radio waves. *Radar* comes from the words *ra*dio *d*etection *a*nd *r*anging.

radiation (ray dee AY shuhn)
Radiation is the giving off of heat, light, or other kinds of energy. For example, heat is radiation from a fire.

rapids (RAP ihds)
Rapids are a quick-moving, often rocky, part of a river.

reef (reef)
A reef is a narrow strip of rock, sand, or coral at or near the surface of the water.

seismograph (SYZ muh graf)
A seismograph is an instrument for recording earthquakes.

Siberia (sy BIHR ee uh)
Siberia is the eastern part of Russia, lying in northern Asia.

sonar (SOH nahr)
Sonar is a device for locating things underwater. *Sonar* comes from the words *so*und *na*vigation and *r*anging.

supernova (soo puhr NOH vuh)
A supernova is a star that explodes, sending tremendous amounts of radiation rushing out into space.

temporary (TEHM puh rehr ee)
Temporary means lasting for only a short time.

trillion (TRIHL yuhn)
A trillion is one thousand billions in the United States and Canada. In Great Britain it is one million billions.

veer (vihr)
To veer means to change direction.

wake (wayk)
The wake is the track a moving ship or any moving object leaves behind it.

Illustration Acknowledgments

The publishers of *Childcraft* gratefully acknowledge the courtesy of the following photographers, agencies, and organizations for illustrations in this volume. When all the illustrations for a sequence of pages are from a single source, the inclusive page numbers are given. Credits should be read from left to right, top to bottom, on their respective pages. All illustrations are the exclusive property of the publishers of *Childcraft* unless names are marked with an asterisk (*).

Cover: Aristocrat and Standard binding—Gregory Manchess
Discovery binding—Roberta Polfus
Heritage binding—Jim Pearson; Richard Hook; Colin Newman; Ted Lewin; Roberta Polfus; Jim Pearson; Gregory Manchess; Jacqueline Rogers; © George Holton, Photo Researchers, Inc.*
1-3: Yoshi Miyake
8 9: Joel Popadics
10-11: David Wenzel
12-13: © World Book Encyclopedia
14-15: © World Book Encyclopedia; David Wenzel
16-17: David Wenzel; Jean Helmer; Academy of Applied Sciences/Photo Trends*
18-19: Academy of Applied Sciences/Photo Trends*
20-21: David Wenzel
22-23: Robert Byrd
24-31: Ted Lewin
32-33: Ted Lewin; Douglas Kirkland, Sygma*
34-35: ©1968 Rene Dahinden*; © World Book Encyclopedia
36-37: Robert Byrd; Christopher Magadini
38-39: Christopher Magadini
40-41: Jean Helmer
42-43: Marie J. Womack, Courtesy of Roy P. Mackal*; Robert Byrd
44-45: Joel Popadics
46-49: Roberta Polfus
50-53: Jerry Tiritilli
54-55: Jerry Tiritilli; © Lucasfilm Ltd. (LFL) 1983. All rights reserved.*
56-57: Woodfin Camp & Assoc.*
58-59: Copyright © by Universal Pictures, a Division of Universal City Studios, Inc. Courtesy of MCA Publishing Rights, a Division of MCA, Inc.*; Robert Byrd
60-61: Roberta Polfus
62-63: Roberta Polfus; © NRAO/AUI*
64-65: Joel Popadics
66-69: David Wenzel
70-71: Stephen Marchesi
72-73: David Wenzel
74-75: Gordon Kibbee
76-81: Bert Dodson
82-83: Stephen Marchesi
84-85: Taiyo Fishery Co., Ltd*
86-87: Stephen Marchesi
88-89: © Gerald L. Wood*
90-97: Gregory Manchess
98-99: David Wenzel
100-101: Stephen Marchesi
102-103: Bert Dodson
104-105: Joel Popadics
106-111: Jerry Tiritilli
112-113: Mutual UFO Networks, Inc.*; Center for UFO Studies*; 1958 Coral Lorenzen (Center for UFO Studies)*
114-119: Jim Pearson
120-121: Jerry Tiritilli
122-123: Dennis DiCicco;* Jerry Tiritilli
124-125: Robert Byrd; Jack Stockman
126-127: Dept. of Defense*
128-129: Jack Stockman
130-131: Tass from Sovfoto*
132-133: Kenneth W. Fink, Bruce Coleman, Inc.*
134-135: Jack Stockman
136-137: Robert Byrd
138-139: Joel Popadics
140-141: Ted Lewin
142-143: Loren A. McIntyre*; © William E. Shawcross*
144-145: Ted Lewin
146-149: Richard Hook
150-151: Geoff Doré, Bruce Coleman Ltd.*; © Adam Woolfitt, Woodfin Camp & Assoc.*
152-153: Richard Hook
154-155: Gordon Kibbee
156-157: Peter Aspery
158-159: Staatliche Museen zu Berlin DDR*
160-163: Jacqueline Rogers
164-165: © Douglas Mazonowicz, Gallery of Prehistoric Art*; Renee Burri, Magnum*
166-167: Jacqueline Rogers
168-169: Joel Popadics
170-171: John Francis
172-175: Jean Helmer
176-177: John Francis
178-181: Colin Newman
182-183: Jean Helmer
184-185: Colin Newman
186-187: John Francis
188-189: Robert Byrd
190-191: World Book photo
192-193: Neg. no. 35608, Photo: Anderson Department Library Services, American Museum of Natural History*; Robert Byrd
194-195: Joel Popadics
196-201: Bill Ersland
202-203: © Andrew Rakoczy, Bruce Coleman Inc.*; Gordon Kibbee
204-209: Bill Ersland
210-219: Richard Hook
220-225: Bill Ersland
226-227: © Mary Crutchfield, Southern Light*
228-229: Jim Pearson
230-231: By courtesy of Merle Greene Robertson. Copyright © 1982 *Ancient Maya Civilization* by Norman Hammond. Rutgers University Press. All rights reserved.
232-233: Gary Gianni
234-235: Jacqueline Rogers
236-237: Jacqueline Rogers; © Rick Frehsee, The Water House, Inc.*
238-239: Jacqueline Rogers; Gordon Kibbee
240-241: Joel Popadics
242-243: Robert Baxter
244-245: © Peter G. Veit*
246-249: Hal Frenck
250-251: © M. & J. Lynch, Sheridan Photo Library*
252-253: Hal Frenck; Granger Collection*
254-255: Hal Frenck
256-257: John Levis from T. A. Reyman, Mount Carmel Mercy Hospital*; Hal Frenck
258-259: Gordon Kibbee; Bert Dodson
260-261: Fotomas Index*
262-267: Bert Dodson
268-269: Gerald Cubitt, Bruce Coleman Ltd.*
270-271: Gary Gianni
272-273: Roberta Polfus
274-275: Roberta Polfus; NASA*
276-277: Gary Gianni
278-279: Field Museum of Natural History*; Gordon Kibbee
280-285: Ted Lewin
286-289: Jaz Szygiel
290-291: Jim Pearson; © George Dineen, Photo Researchers, Inc.*; © George Holton, Photo Researchers, Inc.*
292-293: © Axel Poignant*

Index

This index is an alphabetical list of the important topics covered in this book. It will help you find information given in both words *and* pictures. To help you understand what an entry means, there is often a helping word in parentheses. For example, **Allosaurus** (dinosaur). If there is information in both words and pictures, you will see the words *with pictures* after the page number. If there is *only* a picture, you will see the word *picture* before the page number.